The Gen X Series

NSO

OLYMPIAD WORKBOOK

NATIONAL SCIENCE OLYMPIAD

- **01** Learning Objectives
- **02** Multiple Choice Questions
- **03** HOTS (Achievers Section)
- **04** Model Test Paper
- **05** Answer Keys and Solutions
- **06** OMR Answer Sheet

V&S PUBLISHERS

Published by:

V&S PUBLISHERS

F-2/16, Ansari road, Daryaganj, New Delhi-110002
☎ 23240026, 23240027 • *Fax:* 011-23240028
✉ info@vspublishers.com • 🌐 www.vspublishers.com

 **Online Brandstore: amazon.in/vspublishers**

Regional Office : Hyderabad
5-1-707/1, Brij Bhawan (Beside Central Bank of India Lane)
Bank Street, Koti, Hyderabad - 500 095
☎ 040-24737290
✉ vspublishershyd@gmail.com

Follow us on:   

BUY OUR BOOKS FROM: AMAZON   FLIPKART

© **Copyright:** V&S PUBLISHERS
ISBN 978-81-977761-3-7
New Edition

DISCLAIMER

While every attempt has been made to provide accurate and timely information in this book, neither the author nor the publisher assumes any responsibility for errors, unintended omissions or commissions detected therein. The author and publisher makes no representation or warranty with respect to the comprehensiveness or completeness of the contents provided.

All matters included have been simplified under professional guidance for general information only, without any warranty for applicability on an individual. Any mention of an organization or a website in the book, by way of citation or as a source of additional information, doesn't imply the endorsement of the content either by the author or the publisher. It is possible that websites cited may have changed or removed between the time of editing and publishing the book.

Results from using the expert opinion in this book will be totally dependent on individual circumstances and factors beyond the control of the author and the publisher.

It makes sense to elicit advice from well informed sources before implementing the ideas given in the book. The reader assumes full responsibility for the consequences arising out from reading this book.

For proper guidance, it is advisable to read the book under the watchful eyes of parents/guardian. The buyer of this book assumes all responsibility for the use of given materials and information.

The copyright of the entire content of this book rests with the author/publisher. Any infringement/transmission of the cover design, text or illustrations, in any form, by any means, by any entity will invite legal action and be responsible for consequences thereon.

PUBLISHER'S NOTE

V&S Publishers has carved a significant niche in the publishing industry over the last decade, having successfully published more than 1000 titles across 9 languages spanning over 50 subject categories. Being known for the quality of content, we have built a reputation of excellence and reliability. We have consistently delivered **"Value & Substance"** to our readers, through a wide range of titles across a variety of genres covering school books, fiction and non-fiction that caters to different people from every section of the society.

The **Olympiad Guidebooks for classes 1-10** across all subjects, launched almost a decade ago, under the **GEN X Imprint**, became a go-to-source for the school students in no time, owing to their invaluable and substantive content written in a guidebook pattern,.

Having successfully sold a million copies of the same and in response to demand by both students as well as shopkeepers nationwide; we now present before you our newly launched **Olympiad Workbook Series**, designed for **classes 1-10 across 4 subjects**.

The workbooks are meticulously curated by a team of experienced educators, researchers and subject matter experts, edited by professionals and peer reviewed by teachers. The team has poured its efforts and expertise into creating a crisp and concise workbook which will help and guide the students to the path of success in Olympiad exams. The **MCQs** identified will not only help in scoring top marks in Olympiads but also inculcate a sense of deeper understanding of the subject, by way of solving **HOTS** and referring to complete solutions at the end of the book.

Here we present our new release– **OLYMPIAD WORKBOOK (NSO) CLASS–7** having following features:

- ☞ Based on the latest syllabi
- ☞ MCQs with comprehensive coverage of topics
- ☞ HOTS Questions liberally included
- ☞ A dedicated chapter on logical reasoning
- ☞ Model test paper for thorough practice
- ☞ Sample OMR sheet for real time simulation

We have made sure through our best efforts, that this workbook strictly follows the latest syllabi and patterns of the Olympiad Examination.

As **V&S Publishers** continuously strive to enhance the readability and maintain the credibility of our academic publications, we seek the support of our valuable readers in influencing and enriching the lives of future generations of students.

P.S. While every care has been taken to ensure the correctness of the content, if you come across any error, howsoever minor, do not hesitate to discuss with teachers while pointing that out to us in no uncertain terms.

We wish you all the best for your exams!

DISTINCTIVE FEATURES

01 — Learning Objectives

They list the whole chapter as subtopics, helping the teachers to guide children in a step-by-step manner.

02 — Multiple Choice Questions

MCQs act as an excellent learning aid, helping you to understand and work on your mistakes.

03 — HOTS (Achievers Section)

The High Order Thinking Questions aim to help the student to solve Application-based questions and gain practical understanding of the subject.

04 — Model Test Paper

Model test paper are provided at the end of each book, which help the student to test the knowledge which they have gained after thorough reading of all chapters.

05 — Answer Key

Detailed Answer Key along with explanations aid the pupil to indentify, understand the mistakes they make during the course of Olympiad preparation.

CONTENTS

NUTRITION IN PLANTS AND ANIMALS

LEARNING OBJECTIVES

➤ Nutrition and understand the role of nutrients
➤ The mode of nutrition in plants and animals
➤ The mode of nutrition in amoeba

MULTIPLE CHOICE QUESTIONS

1. A four chambered stomach is present in __________.
   (A) Lion   (B) Crocodile
   (C) Horse   (D) Human

2. Saprophytes obtain their food from __________.
   (A) green plants
   (B) non-green plants
   (C) decaying wastes
   (D) all of these

3. Raw materials used for photosynthesis are __________.
   (A) carbon dioxide
   (B) water
   (C) both (A) and (B)
   (D) none

4. Leaves have a network of veins to transport materials in them, the correct pair is __________.
   (A) veins : road
   (B) veins : pavement
   (C) veins : speed breaker
   (D) veins : bridge

5. Plants get nitrogen from __________.
   (A) air   (B) soil
   (C) animals   (D) all of these

6. Soil in which insectivorous plants grow is deficient in __________.
   (A) phosphorus   (B) sulphur
   (C) nitrogen   (D) all of these

7. The correct photosynthetic equation is __________.
   (A) $\text{Oxygen} + \text{water} \xrightarrow[chlorophyll]{sunlight} \text{Carbon dioxide} + \text{food}$
   (B) $\text{Carbon dioxide} + \text{water} \xrightarrow[chlorophyll]{sunlight} \text{Oxygen} + \text{food}$
   (C) $\text{Carbon dioxide} + \text{water} \rightarrow \text{Oxygen} + \text{food}$
   (D) $\text{Oxygen} + \text{water} \rightarrow \text{Carbon dioxide} + \text{food}$

8. Which of the following is a parasitic plant?
   (A) Saliva   (B) Cactus
   (C) Cuscuta   (D) Cucumber

9. Statement A: All green plants have chlorophyll pigment.
   Statement B: Without chlorophyll, photosynthesis cannot take place.

From the above statements, Shweta concluded that the dark red coloured croton plants in her garden cannot prepare food on its own. But her teacher said it is not true. Why?

(A) Croton plants are green but do not contain chlorophyll.

(B) Croton plants have chlorophyll but it is hidden by dark red colour.

(C) Croton plants are dark red in colour but do not contain chlorophyll.

(D) Croton plants do not have chlorophyll but they can prepare their own food.

10. Housefly takes its food by __________.

(A) biting

(B) chewing

(C) sponging

(D) swallowing

11. Teeth used to grind the apple in mouth are __________.

(A) Incisors

(B) Canines

(C) Premolars and molars

(D) Molars

12. Cellulose forms a large part of the undigested matter we eat. It is __________.

(A) undigested protein

(B) undigested starch

(C) undigested sugar

(D) the substance the cell walls of plants are made of

13. The portion of tongue used to taste sweetness is __________.

(A) tip

(B) centre

(C) sides

(D) back

14. Which of the following are called food factories of the plant?

(A) leaves

(B) stem

(C) roots

(D) flowers

15. The digestion taking place in small intestine is __________.

(A) intracellular

(B) extracellular

(C) both

(D) none

16. An adult has __________ teeth.

(A) 20   (B) 24

(C) 28   (D) 32

17. Match the following __________.

1. Incisors	(A) grinding teeth
2. Canine	(B) cracking teeth
3. Premolars	(C) cutting teeth
4. Molars	(D) tearing teeth

(A) 1 - B, 2 - D, 3 - A, 4 - C

(B) 1 - C, 2 - D, 3 - B, 4 - A

(C) 1 - C, 2 - B, 3 - D, 4 - A

(D) 1 - B, 2 - A, 3 - D, 4 - C

18. Cuscuta lives as a parasite on __________.

(A) pipal   (B) mango

(C) Mirabel   (D) mulberry

19. Xerophytes have very small leaves or spines to __________.

(A) reduce loss of water

(B) reduce volume

(C) reduce weight

(D) look beautiful

20. A plant was kept in a dark room for a week. When its leaves are tested with iodine solution, it did not show the presence of starch. From this experiment it can be concluded that __________ is required for photosynthesis.

(A) iodine

(B) starch

(C) sunlight

(D) darkness

21. Which of the following is a soft material in the tooth?
   (A) root
   (B) pulp
   (C) dentine
   (D) enamel
22. Dentine is __________.
   (A) hard, protective covering on the tooth
   (B) the soft, invisible covering present in a tooth
   (C) the nerve that connects tooth and the brain
   (D) the cavity which contains nerves and blood vessels in a tooth
23. The study of teeth is called __________.
   (A) dentistry   (B) neurology
   (C) cardiology   (D) dermatology
24. Match the columns.

   Column I   **Column II**
   i. Incisors   (A) enzymes
   ii. Food   (B) bile juice
   iii. Cyclosis   (C) cow
   iv. Liver   (D) biting the food
   v. Cud   (E) Amoeba

   (A) i - D, ii - A, iii - E, iv - B, v - C
   (B) i - D, ii - E, iii - B, iv - A, v - C
   (C) i - C, ii - A, iii - D, iv - E, v - B
   (D) i - B, ii - C, iii - A, iv - E, v - D

25. Plants give out water through the pores present under their leaves. The plants living in deserts need to reduce the loss of water because water is very scarce in deserts. Which of the following is an adaptation developed by the desert plants to manage the above situation?
   (A) they do not shed leaves in the summer.
   (B) their leaves are modified into spines.
   (C) they develop roots which come above the ground.
   (D) they have lots of branches and leaves.

HOTS (ACHIEVERS SECTION)

26. Match column I with Column II to show the after digestion processes in human beings.

Column-I	Column-II
i. Carbohydrates	A. Amino acids
ii. Fats	B. Glucose
iii. Proteins	C. Glycerols + Fatty acids

   (A) i–B, ii–C, iii–A
   (B) i–A, ii–C, iii–B
   (C) i–C, ii–B, iii–A
   (D) i–C, ii–A, iii–B

27. Which of the following is a parasitic plant?
   (A) Saliva
   (B) Cuscuta
   (C) Cactus
   (D) Cucumber
28. The bacteria present in root nodules of leguminous plants that fixes the atmospheric nitrogen is ________.
   (A) rhizobium
   (B) nitrifying bacteria
   (C) paramecium
   (D) blue-green algae

29. Various steps of human nutrition are in the order _______.

(A) ingestion, egestion, digestion, assimilation

(B) ingestion, digestion, absorption, assimilation, egestion.

(C) ingestion, absorption, assimilation, egestion, digestion.

(D) ingestion, assimilation, absorption, digestion egestion.

30. Why do we get hiccups while eating?

(A) Due to infection in throat

(B) Due to food particles entering the wind pipe

(C) Due to food particles entering the food pipe

(D) Due to indigestion

1.	Ⓐ Ⓑ Ⓒ Ⓓ	7.	Ⓐ Ⓑ Ⓒ Ⓓ	13.	Ⓐ Ⓑ Ⓒ Ⓓ	19	Ⓐ Ⓑ Ⓒ Ⓓ	25.	Ⓐ Ⓑ Ⓒ Ⓓ
2.	Ⓐ Ⓑ Ⓒ Ⓓ	8.	Ⓐ Ⓑ Ⓒ Ⓓ	14.	Ⓐ Ⓑ Ⓒ Ⓓ	20.	Ⓐ Ⓑ Ⓒ Ⓓ	26.	Ⓐ Ⓑ Ⓒ Ⓓ
3.	Ⓐ Ⓑ Ⓒ Ⓓ	9.	Ⓐ Ⓑ Ⓒ Ⓓ	15.	Ⓐ Ⓑ Ⓒ Ⓓ	21.	Ⓐ Ⓑ Ⓒ Ⓓ	27.	Ⓐ Ⓑ Ⓒ Ⓓ
4.	Ⓐ Ⓑ Ⓒ Ⓓ	10.	Ⓐ Ⓑ Ⓒ Ⓓ	16.	Ⓐ Ⓑ Ⓒ Ⓓ	22.	Ⓐ Ⓑ Ⓒ Ⓓ	28.	Ⓐ Ⓑ Ⓒ Ⓓ
5.	Ⓐ Ⓑ Ⓒ Ⓓ	11.	Ⓐ Ⓑ Ⓒ Ⓓ	17.	Ⓐ Ⓑ Ⓒ Ⓓ	23.	Ⓐ Ⓑ Ⓒ Ⓓ	29.	Ⓐ Ⓑ Ⓒ Ⓓ
6.	Ⓐ Ⓑ Ⓒ Ⓓ	12.	Ⓐ Ⓑ Ⓒ Ⓓ	18.	Ⓐ Ⓑ Ⓒ Ⓓ	24.	Ⓐ Ⓑ Ⓒ Ⓓ	30.	Ⓐ Ⓑ Ⓒ Ⓓ

FIBRE TO FABRIC

LEARNING OBJECTIVES

➤ Natural and synthetic fibres
➤ The processing of fibres into wool
➤ The types of wool
➤ The life cycle of a silkworm
➤ The occupational hazards of silk industry

MULTIPLE CHOICE QUESTIONS

1. An expensive and rare fibre called Cashmere is obtained from _______.
   (A) goat (B) sheep
   (C) camel (D) rabbit

2. The small fluffy fibres are _______.
   (A) reels (B) burrs
   (C) combs (D) bolls

3. Silk moth feed on _______.
   (A) mulberry leaves (B) grape leaves
   (C) eucalyptus leaf (D) Neem leaves

4. Which of these is a synthetic fibre?
   (A) mohair (B) alpaca
   (C) vicuna (D) rayon

5. The life cycle of silkworm is _______.
   (A) eggs, larva, pupa, adult
   (B) eggs, pupa, larva, adult
   (C) eggs, larva, adult, pupa
   (D) none of these

6. Suitable temperature for eggs of silkworm to hatch is _______.
   (A) 20 - 27°C (B) 22 - 27°C
   (C) 25 - 30°C (D) 25 - 31°C

7. Which of the following is the function of hair in animals?
   (A) keeps body cool
   (B) protects internal organs
   (C) trap a lot of heat/air
   (D) give beauty

8. Removal of fleece of sheep with skin is _______.
   (A) refining (B) shearing
   (C) shaving (D) none of these

9. _______ and _______ yield wool found in South America.
   (A) Yak, sheep (B) Goat, sheep
   (C) Llama, Alpaca (D) Angora, goat

10. Rearing of silk worm is _______.
    (A) silviculture (B) sericulture
    (C) apiculture (D) horticulture

11. _______ wool is common in Ladhak and Tibet.
    (A) Yak (B) Sheep
    (C) Goat (D) Camel

12. Silk fabric are prepared from _______.
    (A) silk sheep (B) silk animals
    (C) silk flies (D) silk worms

13. Which of the following has a great tensile strength?
    (A) Wool (B) Cotton
    (C) Silk (D) None of these

14. Which of the following is present in silk fibre?
   (A) lipids
   (B) proteins
   (C) fats
   (D) carbohydrate

15. Which of the following comes in the empty box in the given steps of processing fibres into wool?

   Shearing → ——— → Sorting

   (A) knitting   (B) scouring
   (C) weaving   (D) separating

16. ——— shawls are woven from fur of Kashmiri goat.
   (A) Pashmina   (B) Parse
   (C) Kashmiri   (D) Shimla

17. Match the following.

   A. Scouring   (i) Yields silk fibres
   B. Mulberry   (ii) Cleaning sheared
      leaves   skin
   C. Sheep   (iii) Food of silk worm
   D. Cocoon   (iv) Wool yielding
                            animal

   (A) A - iii, B - i, C - ii, D - iv
   (B) A - ii, B - iii, C - iv, D - i
   (C) A - iv, B - iii, C - ii, D - i
   (D) A - i, B - ii, C - iii, D - iv

18. Which of the following parts swing side to side during the formation of cocoon around the caterpillar?
   (A) abdomen moves
   (B) neck moves
   (C) head moves
   (D) thorax moves

19. Which of the following fibres is spun and woven into woollen cloth?
   (A) shorter fibres
   (B) longer fibres
   (C) fluffy fibres
   (D) none of these

20. In which of the following process threads are taken out from the cocoons?
   (A) shearing
   (B) spinning
   (C) scouring
   (D) reeling

21. Which of the following silk fibre is soft, lustrous and elastic?
   (A) kosa silk
   (B) mulberry silk moth silk
   (C) mooga silk
   (D) tassar silk

22. Which of the following breed yield good quality wool?
   (A) lohi
   (B) Marwari
   (C) patan wadi
   (D) nali

23. You do not get hurt when you get a hair cut. Which of the following is the correct reason?
   (A) hair are dead cells
   (B) the upper layer of the skin with hair is dead
   (C) the roots of hair do not have sensory cells
   (D) all of these

24. Which of the following breeds of sheep are found only in Uttar Pradesh and Himachal Pradesh?
   (A) Nali
   (B) Rampus bushair
   (C) Lohi
   (D) Bakhar wal

25. The larvae of silkworm are called as ———.
   (A) moth
   (B) imago
   (C) nymph
   (D) caterpillar

26. Which of the following is/are not a property of wool?
    (i) It is light weight and can easily be dyed.
    (ii) It is a heat insulator as it can trap a large volume of air.
    (iii) It can not absorb a large amount of water.
    (iv) Wool dissolves in acids and bases.
    (A) (i) and (ii)
    (B) (ii) and (iii)
    (C) (iii) and (iv)
    (D) (i) and (iv)

Directions (27–29): Study the figure given below for obtaining silk fibre from cocoon and answer the following questions.

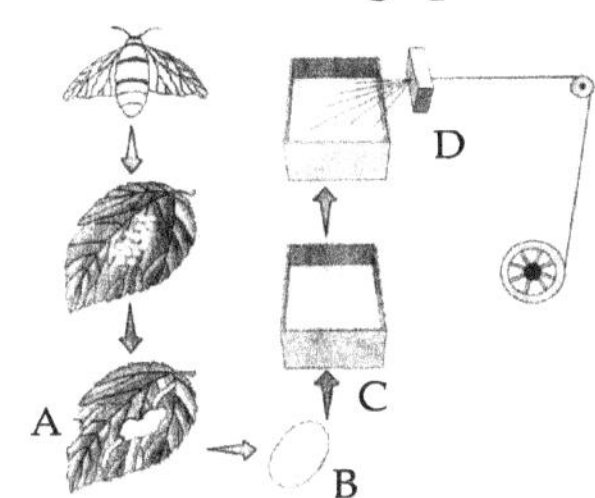

Obtaining Silk Fibre from Cocoon

27. In which of these steps the pupae are killed?
    (A) A
    (B) B
    (C) C
    (D) D

28. In which of these steps caterpillars are formed?
    (A) A
    (B) B
    (C) C
    (D) D

29. In which of these steps silk filament is reeled.
    (A) A
    (B) B
    (C) C
    (D) D

30. Which of the following comes in the empty box in the given steps of processing fibers into wool?

    Shearing $\rightarrow$ Scouring $\rightarrow$?
    (A) Separating
    (B) Sorting
    (C) Weaving
    (D) Knitting

Darken Your Choice with HB Pencil

1.	Ⓐ Ⓑ Ⓒ Ⓓ	7.	Ⓐ Ⓑ Ⓒ Ⓓ	13.	Ⓐ Ⓑ Ⓒ Ⓓ	19	Ⓐ Ⓑ Ⓒ Ⓓ	25.	Ⓐ Ⓑ Ⓒ Ⓓ
2.	Ⓐ Ⓑ Ⓒ Ⓓ	8.	Ⓐ Ⓑ Ⓒ Ⓓ	14.	Ⓐ Ⓑ Ⓒ Ⓓ	20.	Ⓐ Ⓑ Ⓒ Ⓓ	26.	Ⓐ Ⓑ Ⓒ Ⓓ
3.	Ⓐ Ⓑ Ⓒ Ⓓ	9.	Ⓐ Ⓑ Ⓒ Ⓓ	15.	Ⓐ Ⓑ Ⓒ Ⓓ	21.	Ⓐ Ⓑ Ⓒ Ⓓ	27.	Ⓐ Ⓑ Ⓒ Ⓓ
4.	Ⓐ Ⓑ Ⓒ Ⓓ	10.	Ⓐ Ⓑ Ⓒ Ⓓ	16.	Ⓐ Ⓑ Ⓒ Ⓓ	22.	Ⓐ Ⓑ Ⓒ Ⓓ	28.	Ⓐ Ⓑ Ⓒ Ⓓ
5.	Ⓐ Ⓑ Ⓒ Ⓓ	11.	Ⓐ Ⓑ Ⓒ Ⓓ	17.	Ⓐ Ⓑ Ⓒ Ⓓ	23.	Ⓐ Ⓑ Ⓒ Ⓓ	29.	Ⓐ Ⓑ Ⓒ Ⓓ
6.	Ⓐ Ⓑ Ⓒ Ⓓ	12.	Ⓐ Ⓑ Ⓒ Ⓓ	18.	Ⓐ Ⓑ Ⓒ Ⓓ	24.	Ⓐ Ⓑ Ⓒ Ⓓ	30.	Ⓐ Ⓑ Ⓒ Ⓓ

HEAT AND TEMPERATURE

LEARNING OBJECTIVES

➤ Heat and temperature and distinguish them
➤ The temperature of an object
➤ Applications of transfer of heat

MULTIPLE CHOICE QUESTIONS

1. The property of matter of increase in size on heating is called ___________.
   - (A) thermal work
   - (B) thermal energy
   - (C) thermal expansion
   - (D) thermal contraction

2. One glass of water at 40°C is mixed with another glass of water at 60°C. The temperature of mixture will be ________.
   - (A) 40°C
   - (B) 60°C
   - (C) between 40°C and 60°C
   - (D) more than 60°C

3. The degree of hotness or coldness of a body is measured by its ___________.
   - (A) energy
   - (B) radiation
   - (C) heat
   - (D) temperature

4. Mercury is an ideal liquid used in a thermometer because ___________.
   - (A) it expands a lot on heating
   - (B) it does not stick to glass and is visible
   - (C) it has a high boiling temperature
   - (D) all of these

5. At low temperatures _________ type of thermometers is used.
   - (A) water thermometer
   - (B) alcohol thermometer
   - (C) mercury thermometer
   - (D) clinical thermometer

6. 1 cal is equal to ___________.
   - (A) 10 joules
   - (B) 4.18 joules
   - (C) 4.18 dynes
   - (D) none of these

7. The CGS unit for energy is ___________.
   - (A) dyne
   - (B) erg
   - (C) joule
   - (D) centimeter

8. When we touch a steel rod and a paper simultaneously, we feel that the rod is colder because ___________.
   - (A) more heat flows from iron to our body.
   - (B) iron being a good conductor conducts more heat from our body.
   - (C) paper being a good conductor conducts more heat from our body.
   - (D) more heat flows from the paper to our body.

OLYMPIAD WORKBOOK (NSO) CLASS– 7

9. The lower fixed point on the Celsius scale is __________.
   (A) melting point of ice
   (B) boiling point of water
   (C) mean of melting point and boiling point of water
   (D) melting point of mercury

10. In the Celsius scale, the upper fixed point is __________.
    (A) melting point of ice
    (B) boiling point of water
    (C) boiling point of mercury
    (D) mean of melting point and boiling point of water

11. In which of the following, chemical energy is converted into heat energy?
    (A) motor   (B) heater
    (C) candle   (D) refrigerator

12. Handles of cooking utensils should be made of materials that __________.
    (A) radiate heat well
    (B) do not radiate heat
    (C) conduct heat well
    (D) do not conduct heat

13. Which of the following is a good conductor of heat?
    (A) plastic   (B) glass
    (D) water   (D) copper

14. Which of the following is a bad conductor of heat?
    (A) iron   (B) wood
    (C) bronze   (D) aluminium

15. Radiation depends on __________.
    (A) the colour of the substance
    (B) the temperature of the substance
    (C) both (A) and (B)
    (D) none of these

16. Convection of heat takes place in _______.
    (A) metals only
    (B) liquids only
    (C) gases only
    (D) liquids and gases

17. Sea breeze and land breeze __________.
    (A) are caused by the currents set up in air due to conduction.
    (B) are caused by the currents set up in air due to convection.
    (C) are caused by the currents set up in air due to radiation.
    (D) have no relation to conduction, convection and radiation.

18. The incorrect statement is __________.
    (A) convection current causes trade winds.
    (B) transmission of heat without actual movement of particles is called conduction.
    (C) radiation requires medium for heat flow.
    (D) in convection heat is transferred through movement of fluid.

19. A wooden spoon dipped in ice cream cup __________.
    (A) becomes cold by conduction
    (B) becomes cold by convection
    (C) becomes cold by radiation
    (D) does not become cold

20. Find the odd one out __________.
    (A) Good absorbers are good radiators
    (B) Shiny surfaces are good reflectors of heat
    (C) We wear dark-coloured clothes in summers.
    (D) Dark colours are good absorbers of heat.

21. A metal ball is dropped in a beaker containing water at 50°C. Then the heat will __________.
    (A) flow from water to ball
    (B) flow from ball to water
    (C) not flow
    (D) increase the temperature of both ball and water.

22. Reflecting solar films are used on the top of the car to ___________.
   (A) produce electricity
   (B) to absorb more light
   (C) to prevent heating by radiation
   (D) to make it strong

23. The instrument used to detect radiation of heat is ___________.
   (A) thermoscope   (B) barometer
   (C) kinemoscope   (D) stethoscope

24. Gaps are left between railway tracks because ___________.
   (A) gaps hold the tracks firmly
   (B) gaps give the space to the tracks to expand in summer heat
   (C) it is customary to leave the gaps
   (D) to produce gentle rhythmic sound when the train moves on the track.

25. Human body temperature is normally ___________.
   (A) 32°F   (B) 212°F
   (C) 100.4°F   (D) 98.6°F

26. **Statement 1:** The process of transmission of heat energy in solids without actual movement of particles from their position is called conduction.
   Statement 2: In solids particles are very closely packed and have very little space between them.
   (A) Statement 1 is true but statement 2 is false.
   (B) Statement 2 is true but statement 1 is false.
   (C) Both statement 1 and statement 2 are true but statement 2 is not the correct reason for statement 1.
   (D) Both statement 1 and statement 2 are true and statement 2 is the correct reason for statement 1.

27. Given below are the applications of mirror. Which of them are the applications of spherical mirror?
   (i) In making of Kaleidoscope
   (ii) In making of telescope and microscope.
   (iii) In making Periscope.
   (A) Only (i)
   (B) Only (ii)
   (C) Both (i) and (ii)
   (D) All (i), (ii) and (iii)

28. In the Celsius scale, the upper fixed point is ________.
   (A) melting point of ice
   (B) boiling point of mercury
   (C) boiling point of water
   (D) the mean of melting and boiling point of water

29. When same amount of heat is supplied to hydrogen peroxide, iron, and carbon dioxide, which substance expands the most?
   (A) hydrogen peroxide
   (B) carbon dioxide
   (C) iron
   (D) all of these

30. Conduction cannot take place in ________.
   (A) copper
   (B) iron
   (C) aluminum
   (D) vacuum

31. When water is cooled, it contracts until it reaches ________ and then it starts expanding.
   (A) 45°C   (B) 100°C
   (C) 37°C   (D) 4°C

32. Our body temperature is maintained at
_________.
(A) 37°c
(b 100°C
(C) 98°C
(D) 20° C

33. Impurities in water _________.
(A) lower the freezing point
(B) increase the boiling point
(C) none of these
(D) both (A) and (B)

34. A marble tile would feel cold as compared to a wooden tile on a winter morning because the marble tile
(A) is a better conductor of heat than the wooden tile
(B) is polished while wooden tile is not polished
(C) reflects more heat than wooden tile
(D) is a poor conductor of heat than the wooden tile

35. A beggar wrapped himself with a few layers of newspaper on a cold winter night. This helped him to keep himself warm because
(A) friction between the layers of newspaper produces heat
(B) air trapped between the layers of newspaper is a bad conductor of heat
(C) newspaper is a conductor of heat
(D) newspaper is at a higher temperature than the temperature of the surroundings

1. Ⓐ Ⓑ Ⓒ Ⓓ	8. Ⓐ Ⓑ Ⓒ Ⓓ	15. Ⓐ Ⓑ Ⓒ Ⓓ	22 Ⓐ Ⓑ Ⓒ Ⓓ	29. Ⓐ Ⓑ Ⓒ Ⓓ
2. Ⓐ Ⓑ Ⓒ Ⓓ	9. Ⓐ Ⓑ Ⓒ Ⓓ	16. Ⓐ Ⓑ Ⓒ Ⓓ	23. Ⓐ Ⓑ Ⓒ Ⓓ	30. Ⓐ Ⓑ Ⓒ Ⓓ
3. Ⓐ Ⓑ Ⓒ Ⓓ	10. Ⓐ Ⓑ Ⓒ Ⓓ	17. Ⓐ Ⓑ Ⓒ Ⓓ	24. Ⓐ Ⓑ Ⓒ Ⓓ	31. Ⓐ Ⓑ Ⓒ Ⓓ
4. Ⓐ Ⓑ Ⓒ Ⓓ	11. Ⓐ Ⓑ Ⓒ Ⓓ	18. Ⓐ Ⓑ Ⓒ Ⓓ	25. Ⓐ Ⓑ Ⓒ Ⓓ	32. Ⓐ Ⓑ Ⓒ Ⓓ
5. Ⓐ Ⓑ Ⓒ Ⓓ	12. Ⓐ Ⓑ Ⓒ Ⓓ	19. Ⓐ Ⓑ Ⓒ Ⓓ	26. Ⓐ Ⓑ Ⓒ Ⓓ	33. Ⓐ Ⓑ Ⓒ Ⓓ
6. Ⓐ Ⓑ Ⓒ Ⓓ	13. Ⓐ Ⓑ Ⓒ Ⓓ	20. Ⓐ Ⓑ Ⓒ Ⓓ	27. Ⓐ Ⓑ Ⓒ Ⓓ	34. Ⓐ Ⓑ Ⓒ Ⓓ
7. Ⓐ Ⓑ Ⓒ Ⓓ	14. Ⓐ Ⓑ Ⓒ Ⓓ	21. Ⓐ Ⓑ Ⓒ Ⓓ	28. Ⓐ Ⓑ Ⓒ Ⓓ	35. Ⓐ Ⓑ Ⓒ Ⓓ

ACIDS, BASES AND SALTS

LEARNING OBJECTIVES

➤ Indicators – natural and artificial
➤ Salts and neutralization reactions
➤ The importance of neutralization reactions

MULTIPLE CHOICE QUESTIONS

1. Acid present in amla and lemon is __________.
   (A) acetic acid   (B) nitric acid
   (C) citric acid   (D) vinegar

2. Each cell of our body contains this. It is also present in our proteins and fat. What is it?
   (A) acid   (B) base
   (C) salt   (D) none of these

3. Common name of copper sulphate is __________.
   (A) nitra   (B) blue vitriol
   (C) quick lime   (D) chalk

4. $2NaOH + MgSO_4 \rightarrow ?$
   (A) $MgO + Na_2SO_4$
   (B) $Mg(OH)_2 + Na_2SO_4$
   (C) $Mg(OH)_2$
   (D) $MgO + Na_2O + H_2O$

5. What is the common name of sodium carbonate?
   (A) washing soda   (B) blue vitriol
   (C) baking soda   (D) POP

6. Common name of H_2SO_4 is __________.
   (A) blue vitriol   (B) green vitriol
   (C) oil of vitriol   (D) muriatic acid

7. Chemically baking soda is __________.
   (A) Na_2CO_3 (B) $NaHCO_3$
   (C) $Ca(OH)_2$ (D) CaO

8. An indicator is a substance which shows the presence of a chemical substance by __________.
   (A) giving smell
   (B) changing colour
   (C) producing sound
   (D) none

9. Which is not an indicator?
   (A) turmeric   (B) litmus
   (C) HCl   (D) methyl orange

10. Which of the following statements is incorrect?
    (A) acid turns blue litmus red
    (B) base turns red litmus blue
    (C) both (A) and (B)
    (D) water change the colour of a litmus

11. Salt is formed when __________.
    (A) metals react with water
    (B) metals react with oxygen
    (C) base reacts with acid
    (D) none of these

12. Which of the following is a neutralization reaction?

(A) $4Na + O_2 \rightarrow 2Na_2O$
(B) $NaOH + HCl \rightarrow NaCl + H_2O$
(C) $2Ca + O_2 \rightarrow 2CaO$
(D) $Na2O + H_2O \rightarrow 2NaOH$

13. Acid reacts with metal to form _________.
(A) salt + water
(B) salt + CO_2
(C) salt + O_2
(D) salt + H_2

14. When an acid is slowly added to water, _______.
(A) it releases heat
(B) it absorbs heat
(C) there is no heat change
(D) none of these

15. Lime water is a solution of _________.
(A) NaOH in water
(B) NaCl in water
(C) $Ca(OH)_2$ in water
(D) $CaCl_2$ in water

16. The acid used in the making of vinegar is _________.
(A) nitric acid
(B) acetic acid
(C) formic acid
(D) sulphuric acid

17. Caustic potash is the common name of _________.
(A) KOH
(B) NH_4OH
(C) LiOH
(D) $[Al(OH)_3]$

18. Which of the following is a property of a base?
(A) they taste bitter
(B) they turn red litmus blue
(C) they feel soapy to touch
(D) all of these

19. $Mg + H_2SO_4 \rightarrow$?
(A) $MgO + H_2$
(B) $MgSO_4 + O_2$
(C) $MgSO_4 + H_2O$
(D) $MgSO_4 + H_2$

20. The base used in making antacids is _______.
(A) barium hydroxide
(B) sodium hydroxide
(C) calcium hydroxide
(D) magnesium hydroxide

21. In fire extinguishers, the reaction between the carbonate and the acid gives _________.
(A) O_2
(B) CO_2
(C) H_2
(D) Cl_2

22. In acids, methyl orange turns _________.
(A) yellow
(B) white
(C) red
(D) green

23. In bases, methyl orange turns _________.
(A) red
(B) yellow
(C) green
(D) black

24. Acids are formed when _________.
(A) metals combine with oxygen
(B) oxides of non metals dissolve in water
(C) metals react with water
(D) bases dissolve in water

25. Phenolphthalein turns _______ in acidic and neutral solutions.
(A) red
(B) pink
(C) colourless
(D) green

HOTS (ACHIEVERS SECTION)

26. Column I contains the natural sources of acid and Column II contains the type of acid. Match them.

Column-I	Column-II
i. Grapes	A. Malric acid
ii. Unripe green apples	B. Oxalic acid
iii. Spinach	C. Tartaric acid

(A) i–C, ii–B, iii–A
(B) ii–C, i–A, iii–B
(C) i–B, ii–C, iii–A
(D) i–A, ii–B, iii–C

27. The metal which can displace hydrogen from acid is _______.
(A) silver
(B) calcium
(C) mercury
(D) gold

28. $Na_2CO_3 + 2HCl \rightarrow$?
   (A) $2NaCl + CO_2 + H_2O$
   (B) $NaCl + H_2O$
   (C) $NaCl + O_2$
   (D) $NaCl + O_2 + H_2$

29. The metal which can displace zinc from its solution is ________.
   (A) Fe
   (B) Pb
   (C) Cu
   (D) Mg

30. Turmeric is a natural indicator. On adding its paste to acid and base separately, which colours would be observed?
   (A) Yellow in both acid and base
   (B) Yellow in acid and red in base
   (C) Pink in acid and yellow in base
   (D) Red in acid and blue in base

1.	Ⓐ Ⓑ Ⓒ Ⓓ	7.	Ⓐ Ⓑ Ⓒ Ⓓ	13.	Ⓐ Ⓑ Ⓒ Ⓓ	19	Ⓐ Ⓑ Ⓒ Ⓓ	25.	Ⓐ Ⓑ Ⓒ Ⓓ
2.	Ⓐ Ⓑ Ⓒ Ⓓ	8.	Ⓐ Ⓑ Ⓒ Ⓓ	14.	Ⓐ Ⓑ Ⓒ Ⓓ	20.	Ⓐ Ⓑ Ⓒ Ⓓ	26.	Ⓐ Ⓑ Ⓒ Ⓓ
3.	Ⓐ Ⓑ Ⓒ Ⓓ	9.	Ⓐ Ⓑ Ⓒ Ⓓ	15.	Ⓐ Ⓑ Ⓒ Ⓓ	21.	Ⓐ Ⓑ Ⓒ Ⓓ	27.	Ⓐ Ⓑ Ⓒ Ⓓ
4.	Ⓐ Ⓑ Ⓒ Ⓓ	10.	Ⓐ Ⓑ Ⓒ Ⓓ	16.	Ⓐ Ⓑ Ⓒ Ⓓ	22.	Ⓐ Ⓑ Ⓒ Ⓓ	28.	Ⓐ Ⓑ Ⓒ Ⓓ
5.	Ⓐ Ⓑ Ⓒ Ⓓ	11.	Ⓐ Ⓑ Ⓒ Ⓓ	17.	Ⓐ Ⓑ Ⓒ Ⓓ	23.	Ⓐ Ⓑ Ⓒ Ⓓ	29.	Ⓐ Ⓑ Ⓒ Ⓓ
6.	Ⓐ Ⓑ Ⓒ Ⓓ	12.	Ⓐ Ⓑ Ⓒ Ⓓ	18.	Ⓐ Ⓑ Ⓒ Ⓓ	24.	Ⓐ Ⓑ Ⓒ Ⓓ	30.	Ⓐ Ⓑ Ⓒ Ⓓ

PHYSICAL AND CHEMICAL CHANGES

5

➤ Physical and chemical change
➤ Rusting of iron as a chemical change
➤ Differences between physical and chemical changes

MULTIPLE CHOICE QUESTIONS

1. Burning of wood is a _________ change.
   - (A) physical
   - (B) chemical
   - (C) reversible
   - (D) all of these

2. Neutralization change is a _________.
   - (A) chemical change
   - (B) physical change
   - (C) sometimes physical and sometimes chemical change
   - (D) neither physical nor chemical change

3. What is the main cause of acid rain?
   - (A) afforestation
   - (B) deforestation
   - (C) pollution
   - (D) excessive rains

4. Some pieces of chalk were taken and mixed with water. In this change, how many new substances are formed?
   - (A) 1
   - (B) 2
   - (C) 3
   - (D) no new substance is formed

5. Two changes are stated below _________.
   - (i) a piece of magnesium gives out bright flames when burnt.
   - (ii) a piece of iron glows red when heated strongly.

   Which of these is a chemical change?
   - (A) (i) only
   - (B) (ii) only
   - (C) both (i) and (ii)
   - (D) neither (i) nor (ii)

6. Which of the following changes is not a chemical change?
   - (A) boiling of egg
   - (B) boiling of water
   - (C) burning of cloth
   - (D) burning of paper

7. Which of the following Venn diagrams shows the relationship between changes correctly?

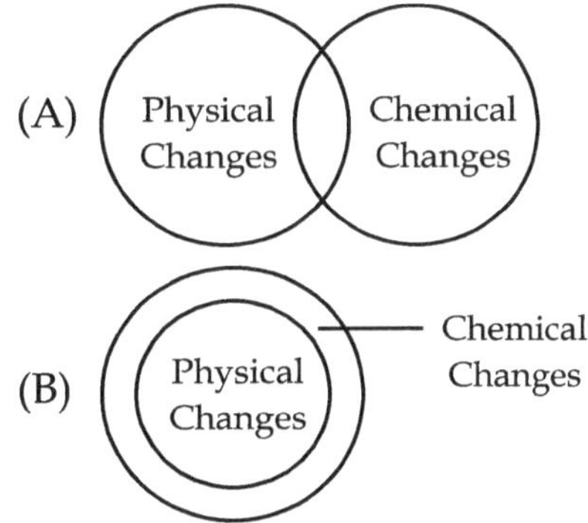

(C) 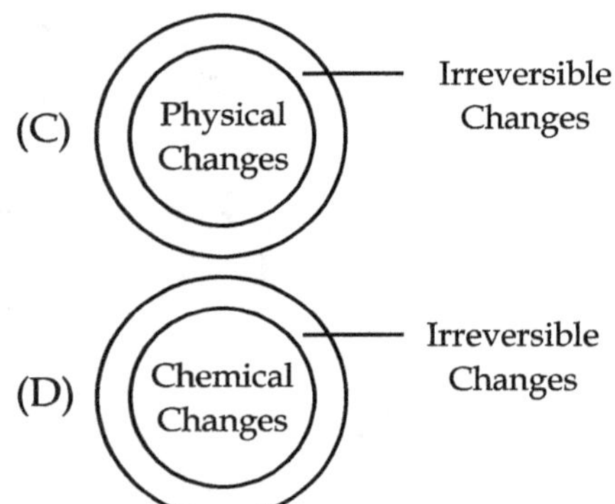

Physical Changes — Irreversible Changes

(D) Chemical Changes — Irreversible Changes

8. Which one is a physical change?
   (A) cooking of food
   (B) melting of wax
   (C) rusting of iron
   (D) curdling of milk

9. When iron pieces are added to a blue colour copper sulphate solution, the colour of copper sulphate changes to __________.
   (A) green
   (B) brown
   (C) blue black
   (D) none of these

10. The gas released when vinegar is mixed with baking soda is __________.
    (A) O_2 (B) H_2
    (C) NO_2 (D) CO_2

11. Which of the following is not a physical change?
    (A) freezing water into ice
    (B) tearing a paper
    (C) bending an iron rod
    (D) none of these

12. Manisha took a little bit of soil from her garden and mixed it with water. When she dipped blue litmus in it, the litmus turned red. By adding which of following to her garden will she get better plant growth?
    (A) water
    (B) salt
    (C) slaked lime
    (D) hydrochloric acid

13. Three substances given below are kept in the open for a few days and some changes were observed.

Eggs   Bottle   Moth balls

Which of the substances will show chemical changes?
   (A) eggs
   (B) plastic bottle
   (C) both eggs and moth balls
   (D) eggs, plastic bottle and moth balls

14. Pooja took a candle in a vessel and heated the vessel. Even though the candle did not burn, it changed its shape and state. What kind of change is this?
    (A) chemical change
    (B) physical change
    (C) naturalization
    (D) none of these

15. The product formed when Mg is burnt in air is __________.
    (A) MgO (B) MgO_2
    (C) $Mg(OH)_2$ (D) Mg_2O_2

16. Rusting takes place in __________.
    (A) air-free moisture
    (B) moisture-free air
    (C) moist air
    (D) none of these

17. Which of the following is an antacid?
    (A) H_2O (B) $Mg(OH)_2$
    (C) $NaOH$ (D) H_2SO_4

18. Adding sodium chloride to water is a __________.
    (A) physical change
    (B) chemical change
    (C) chemical reaction
    (D) none of these

Direction (19-24): Three different substances were taken and tested with litmus paper. The results are given below. Based on the results answer the questions.

Substance	X	Y	Z
Red litmus	Turns blue	No change	No change
Blue litmus	No change	Turns red	No change

19. What could be the substance X?
    (A) salt
    (B) water
    (C) base
    (D) acid
20. What could be the substance Y?
    (A) acid
    (B) base
    (C) water
    (D) salt
21. What could be the substance Z?
    (A) salt
    (B) water
    (C) either (A) and (B)
    (D) base
22. How can you obtain the substance Z?
    (A) by dissolving X in water
    (B) by dissolving Y in water
    (C) by the reaction of X and Y
    (D) cannot be said
23. Which of the following could be the substance Z
    (A) H_2O
    (B) HNO_3
    (C) H_2SO_4
    (D) KOH
24. How will the substance X behave with phenolphthalein?
    (A) turns blue
    (B) turns red
    (C) turns pink
    (D) remains colourless
25. Which of the following are not paired correctly?
    (A) Calamine - Zinc carbonate
    (B) Slaked lime - Calcium oxide
    (C) Baking soda - Sodium hydrogen carbonate
    (D) Common salt - Sodium chloride
26. Glowing of an electric bulb is a _____ change.
    (A) physical
    (B) chemical
    (C) both (A) and (B)
    (D) none of these
27. The formula of rust is _______.
    (A) FeO
    (B) Fe_2O
    (C) Fe_2O_3
    (D) Fe_3O_4
28. The process of separating a pure substance in the form of crystals from the hot saturated solution by cooling is called _______.
    (A) distillation
    (B) crystallization
    (C) condensation
    (D) evaporation
29. Limewater turning milky in presence of CO_2 is _______.
    (A) physical change
    (B) chemical change
    (C) both (A) and (B)
    (D) none
30. The crystals that are obtained after crystallization are _______.
    (A) 10% pure
    (B) between 50% to 90% pure
    (C) between 20% to 50% pure
    (D) more than 90% pure

31. Which of the following is not a chemical change?
    (A) Rusting of iron
    (B) Burning of paper
    (C) Digestion of food
    (D) Precipitation of rain and snow

32. When you put a candle in a vessel and heat the vessel, you will observe that the candle does not burn, it changes its shape and state. What kind of change is this?
    (A) Physical change
    (B) Chemical change
    (C) Naturalistion
    (D) None of these

33. Which of the following are true when milk changes into curd?
    (i) Its state is changed from liquid to semi-solid.
    (ii) It changes colour.
    (iii) It changes taste.
    (iv) The change cannot be reversed.
    Choose the correct option.
    (A) (i) and (ii)   (B) (ii) and (iii)
    (C) (i), (iii) and (iv)   (D) (i) to (iv)

34. A man painted his main gate made up of iron, to
    (i)   prevent it from rusting.
    (ii) protect it from the sun.
    (iii) make it look beautiful.
    (iv) make it dust free.
    Which of the above statements is/are correct?
    (A) (i) and (ii)   (B) (ii) and (iii)
    (C) Only (ii)   (D) (i) and (iii)

35. Iron pillar near the Qutub Minar in Delhi is famous for the following facts. Which of these facts is responsible for its long stability?
    (A) It is more than 7 m high.
    (B) It weighs about 6000 kg.
    (C) It was built more than 1600 years ago.
    (D) It has not rusted after such a long period of existence.

Darken Your Choice with HB Pencil

1.	Ⓐ Ⓑ Ⓒ Ⓓ	8.	Ⓐ Ⓑ Ⓒ Ⓓ	15.	Ⓐ Ⓑ Ⓒ Ⓓ	22	Ⓐ Ⓑ Ⓒ Ⓓ	29.	Ⓐ Ⓑ Ⓒ Ⓓ
2.	Ⓐ Ⓑ Ⓒ Ⓓ	9.	Ⓐ Ⓑ Ⓒ Ⓓ	16.	Ⓐ Ⓑ Ⓒ Ⓓ	23.	Ⓐ Ⓑ Ⓒ Ⓓ	30.	Ⓐ Ⓑ Ⓒ Ⓓ
3.	Ⓐ Ⓑ Ⓒ Ⓓ	10.	Ⓐ Ⓑ Ⓒ Ⓓ	17.	Ⓐ Ⓑ Ⓒ Ⓓ	24.	Ⓐ Ⓑ Ⓒ Ⓓ	31.	Ⓐ Ⓑ Ⓒ Ⓓ
4.	Ⓐ Ⓑ Ⓒ Ⓓ	11.	Ⓐ Ⓑ Ⓒ Ⓓ	18.	Ⓐ Ⓑ Ⓒ Ⓓ	25.	Ⓐ Ⓑ Ⓒ Ⓓ	32.	Ⓐ Ⓑ Ⓒ Ⓓ
5.	Ⓐ Ⓑ Ⓒ Ⓓ	12.	Ⓐ Ⓑ Ⓒ Ⓓ	19.	Ⓐ Ⓑ Ⓒ Ⓓ	26.	Ⓐ Ⓑ Ⓒ Ⓓ	33.	Ⓐ Ⓑ Ⓒ Ⓓ
6.	Ⓐ Ⓑ Ⓒ Ⓓ	13.	Ⓐ Ⓑ Ⓒ Ⓓ	20.	Ⓐ Ⓑ Ⓒ Ⓓ	27.	Ⓐ Ⓑ Ⓒ Ⓓ	34.	Ⓐ Ⓑ Ⓒ Ⓓ
7.	Ⓐ Ⓑ Ⓒ Ⓓ	14.	Ⓐ Ⓑ Ⓒ Ⓓ	21.	Ⓐ Ⓑ Ⓒ Ⓓ	28.	Ⓐ Ⓑ Ⓒ Ⓓ	35.	Ⓐ Ⓑ Ⓒ Ⓓ

WEATHER, CLIMATE AND ADAPTATIONS OF ANIMALS

6

LEARNING OBJECTIVES

➤ Weather forecasting
➤ Weather and climate
➤ Adaptations in animals of different regions

MULTIPLE CHOICE QUESTIONS

1. Climate of a place is affected by ————.
   (A) altitude of a place
   (B) distance from the sea
   (C) location of a place
   (D) all of these

2. The trunk of an elephant is a modification of the ————.
   (A) lower lip and nose
   (B) upper lip and nose
   (C) lower jaw and nose
   (D) upper jaw and nose

3. Adjustment of plants and animals to environmental changes is called ————.
   (A) mimicry
   (B) aestivation
   (C) adaptation
   (D) hibernation

4. A student identified the following characteristics in an animal ————.
   (i) ability to climb the trees
   (ii) spines to prevent from slipping
   (iii) strong claws and broad hip girdles
   Which of the following titles best suits the above animal?
   (A) amphibian
   (B) arboreal animal
   (C) aquatic animal
   (D) terrestrial animal

5. Earth's position in solar system is ————.
   (A) 1st nearest to the sun
   (B) 2nd nearest to the sun
   (C) 3rd nearest to the sun
   (D) 4th nearest to the sun

6. Which of the following animals have long sticky tongues?
   (A) eagles
   (B) chameleon
   (C) cheetahs
   (D) cows

7. Which of the following statements is false?
   (A) In cold regions plants grow new leaves during winter.
   (B) Some desert plants do not have leaves.
   (C) Thick skin protects the animals from the blazing heat of the sun.
   (D) Bears have thick fur as a protection against the cold.

8. Red-eyed frog and New world monkey are animals of ___________.
   (A) forest
   (B) desert
   (C) tropical forest
   (D) tropical rainforest

9. Which of the following do penguins adapt to live in extremely cold conditions?
   (A) a white colour thick skin and less fat
   (B) white body, paws for swimming, gills for respiration
   (C) thin skin, large eyes, white fur
   (D) white colour, thick skin and a lot of fat

10. Presence of sharp claws and powerful feet in the fishing eagle is an adaptation for ___________.
    (A) climate
    (B) self protection
    (C) food
    (D) changing environment

11. Match the following.

    (A) Toucan bird   (I)   modified teeth
    (B) Siberian bird   (II) Silver white mane
    (C) Tusk of   (III) Long beak
        elephant
    (D) Macaque   (IV) migrate to India during winter

    (A) A - I, B - II, C - III, D - IV
    (B) A - IV, B - III, C - II, D - I
    (C) A - III, B - IV, C - I, D - II
    (D) A - III, B - I, C - II, D - IV

12. Which of the following animals have sticky pads on its feet?
    (A) green eyed frog
    (B) blue eyed frog
    (C) red eyed frog
    (D) yellow eyed frog

13. The rain gauge is used to measure ___________.
    (A) rain water
    (B) rainfall
    (C) rain region
    (D) rain speed

14. The size of morning sun is ___________.
    (A) small
    (B) very small
    (C) big
    (D) very big in comparison to day's sun

15. An adaptation to arboreal life (tree living) is ___________.
    (A) camouflage
    (B) opposable thumb
    (C) hibernation
    (D) thick skin

16. Which of the following departments prepare weather reports?
    (A) health department
    (B) environment department
    (C) pollution department
    (D) meteorological department

17. Weather is predicted by considering ___________.
    (A) amount of water vapour
    (B) the movement of air
    (C) temperature
    (D) all of these

18. ___________ maintains balance in a monkey.
    (A) Legs
    (B) Tail
    (C) Hands
    (D) None of these

19. Sheep in ________ region have thicker fur than the sheep living in ________ region.
    (A) cold, warm
    (B) warm, hot
    (C) hot, warm
    (D) warm, cold

20. The scaly skin of snakes __________.
   (A) helps them to crawl
   (B) makes them beautiful
   (C) scares human beings
   (D) protects them from drying
21. An animal is taken to polar region. Which of the following adaptive characteristics may help it to survive in the new environment?
   (A) sharp beaks and strong claws
   (B) growth of thick fur on its skin
   (C) light weight wings to fly
   (D) growth of thick and less hairy skin
22. The adaptation mechanism of chameleon is __________.
   (A) to develop scaly skin on its body to maintain moisture
   (B) to migrate to long distance in the winter
   (C) changing colours on its body to maintain moisture
   (D) to hibernate in the winter

23. Study the following adaptations __________.
   (A) white fur is not easily visible in the snowy white background
   (B) long, curved and sharp claws help to walk on ice
   (C) very strong sense of smell to locate its prey
   These are the adaptations of a __________.
   (A) bear   (B) camel
   (C) penguin   (D) polar bear
24. Plants in cold regions shed leaves during __________ season.
   (A) rainy   (B) winter
   (C) spring   (D) summer
25. Travelling long distances to avoid hardships of winter is called __________.
   (A) migration
   (B) aestivation
   (C) adaptation
   (D) hibernation

HOTS (ACHIEVERS SECTION)

26. Consider the following adaptations:
   (i) Streamlined body
   (A) Scales on skin
   (b   Presence of gills
   These adaptations are found in:
   (A) Aboreal animals
   (B) Amphibians
   (C) Aquatic animals
   (D) Terestial animals
27. The maximum and minimum tempera-tures displayed daily in the weather bulletin refer to the:
   (A) highest day temperature and lowest night temperature of the day
   (B) highest day temperature and highest night temperature of the month
   (C) temperature recorded at 12 noon and at mid night (00.00 h)
   (D) average highest temperature of day and average lowest temperature of night

28. Out of the given definitions, which is the most appropriate definition of climate?
   (A) Changes in weather conditions in a year
   (B) Average weather pattern of many years
   (C) Change in weather pattern in a few years
   (D) Weather conditions during summer

29. Red-eyed frog have __________.
   (A) small eyes   (B) green eyes
   (C) bulging eyes   (D) no-eyes

30. Paheli went to a wildlife sanctuary, where she saw dense vegetation of trees, shrubs, herbs and also a variety of animals like monkeys, birds, elephants, snakes, frogs, etc. The most likely location of this sanctuary is in the ______.
   (A) temperate region
   (B) tropical region
   (C) polar region
   (D) coastal region

-Darken Your Choice with HB Pencil-

1.	Ⓐ Ⓑ Ⓒ Ⓓ	7.	Ⓐ Ⓑ Ⓒ Ⓓ	13.	Ⓐ Ⓑ Ⓒ Ⓓ	19	Ⓐ Ⓑ Ⓒ Ⓓ	25.	Ⓐ Ⓑ Ⓒ Ⓓ
2.	Ⓐ Ⓑ Ⓒ Ⓓ	8.	Ⓐ Ⓑ Ⓒ Ⓓ	14.	Ⓐ Ⓑ Ⓒ Ⓓ	20.	Ⓐ Ⓑ Ⓒ Ⓓ	26.	Ⓐ Ⓑ Ⓒ Ⓓ
3.	Ⓐ Ⓑ Ⓒ Ⓓ	9.	Ⓐ Ⓑ Ⓒ Ⓓ	15.	Ⓐ Ⓑ Ⓒ Ⓓ	21.	Ⓐ Ⓑ Ⓒ Ⓓ	27.	Ⓐ Ⓑ Ⓒ Ⓓ
4.	Ⓐ Ⓑ Ⓒ Ⓓ	10.	Ⓐ Ⓑ Ⓒ Ⓓ	16.	Ⓐ Ⓑ Ⓒ Ⓓ	22.	Ⓐ Ⓑ Ⓒ Ⓓ	28.	Ⓐ Ⓑ Ⓒ Ⓓ
5.	Ⓐ Ⓑ Ⓒ Ⓓ	11.	Ⓐ Ⓑ Ⓒ Ⓓ	17.	Ⓐ Ⓑ Ⓒ Ⓓ	23.	Ⓐ Ⓑ Ⓒ Ⓓ	29.	Ⓐ Ⓑ Ⓒ Ⓓ
6.	Ⓐ Ⓑ Ⓒ Ⓓ	12.	Ⓐ Ⓑ Ⓒ Ⓓ	18.	Ⓐ Ⓑ Ⓒ Ⓓ	24.	Ⓐ Ⓑ Ⓒ Ⓓ	30.	Ⓐ Ⓑ Ⓒ Ⓓ

WINDS, STORMS AND CYCLONES

LEARNING OBJECTIVES

➤ Natural phenomena
➤ Storms, thunderstorms, cyclones and tornadoes
➤ Safety precautions during natural disaster

MULTIPLE CHOICE QUESTIONS

1. Which of the following will rises the highest?
   (A) air at 10°C   (B) air at 20°C
   (C) air at 40°C   (D) air at –5°C

2. An anemometer is an instrument that is most similar to a _______.
   (A) flag   (B) electric meter
   (C) accelerator   (D) speedometer

3. Cold winds usually show _______ movements, while warm winds usually show _______ movements.
   (A) lateral, vertical   (B) vertical, lateral
   (C) lateral, lateral   (D) vertical, vertical

4. When a vehicle moves very fast, a/an _______ is created temporarily behind it.
   (A) eye   (B) cyclone
   (C) low pressure   (D) high pressure

5. Which of the following statements is incorrect?
   (A) rain, thunder and lightening are natural phenomena.
   (B) slow moving air is called wind.
   (C) high speed winds are accompanied by reduced air pressure.
   (D) earthquake, landslide and tsunami happen due to geological changes.

6. On heating, gases become _______ because the molecules _______.
   (A) heavier, contract
   (B) heavier, expand
   (C) lighter, contract
   (D) lighter, expand

7. The monsoon winds that carry a lot of water to India come from the _______.
   (A) northeast   (B) northwest
   (C) southeast   (D) southwest

8. During the formation of rain, when water vapour changes back to liquid in the form of rain drops _______.
   (A) heat is released
   (B) heat is absorbed
   (C) heat is first absorbed and then released
   (D) there is no exchange of heat.

9. Which of the following is the best thing to do during heavy lightning?
   (A) going into the nearest water body
   (B) standing under a tall tree
   (C) lying on the ground in an open place
   (D) staying indoors, away from metallic doors or windows

10. How do cyclones decrease the fertility of the soil in the coastal areas?
    (A) by flooding the land with saline water.
    (B) by decreasing the water table of the place.
    (C) by dissolving soil and rocks
    (D) by increasing the water table of the place.

11. Which of the following is the first sign of an approaching cyclone?
    (A) powerful water waves
    (B) cool breeze and rains
    (C) high temperature and humidity
    (D) rains accompanied by lightning

12. The winds on the earth do not flow in the exact "north to south" or "south to north" directions because _______.
    (A) of the shape of the earth
    (B) of the rotation of the earth
    (C) of the seasons of the earth
    (D) all of these

13. Sea and land breezes are caused because of _______.
    (A) rains   (B) conduction
    (C) convection   (D) cyclones

14. Which of the following doesn't show that air has pressure?
    (A) flying a kite
    (B) riding a bicycle against the wind
    (C) ball falling to the ground
    (D) drinking a soft drink through a straw

15. During the take-off of an aeroplane there is a _______ pressure on the top and a _______ pressure below.
    (A) low, low   (B) low, high
    (C) high, high   (D) high, low

16. Which condition is necessary for the development of cyclonic storm?
    (A) atmospheric instability
    (B) high relative humidity
    (C) a warm sea temperature
    (D) all of these

17. Which country is most likely to be affected by cyclones?
    (A) Hungry   (B) Indonesia
    (C) Mongolia   (D) Nepal

18. While drinking a soft drink with the help of a straw, the pressure in the straw is _______ and the pressure in the bottle is _______.
    (A) less, less   (B) less, high
    (C) high, less   (D) high, high

19. Which of the following is most likely to be in the 'eye' of a cyclone?
    (A) It has high speed winds.
    (B) It is an area of a low pressure.
    (C) It is an area of high pressure.
    (D) It has lots of clouds and rains.

20. What is the best thing to do when strong winds are blowing over a hut having a weak thatched roof?
    (A) open the doors and windows
    (B) make holes in the roof
    (C) burn wood inside
    (D) close all the doors and windows

21. On the earth wind from the north and the south blow towards the equator. From this, we can understand that _______.
    (A) it is hotter in and around the north and the south.
    (B) it is hotter in and around the equator.
    (C) wind doesn't flow from the east or the west.
    (D) earth is round or spherical in shape.

22. Which one of the following statements is correct about air?
    (A) air is made of gases
    (B) warm air rises up
    (C) air blows from high pressure area to low pressure area
    (D) all of these

23. Air pressure on the Mount Everest with respect to sea level is _______.
    (A) greater   (B) smaller
    (C) equal   (D) none of there

24. The earth's atmosphere is layered according to the availability of gases, temperature and altitude. Which one of the following layers is found between

the thermosphere and stratosphere?
(A) exosphere   (B) mesosphere
(C) troposphere   (D) inosphere

25. Cooler air from 0 to 30 degree latitudes on either side of the equator moves in towards the equator. These winds blow towards the equator from:

(A) North to south in northern hemisphere
(B) South to north in northern hemisphere
(C) East to west
(D) West to east

HOTS (ACHIEVERS SECTION)

26. **Statement 1:** A cyclone is a violent, dark funnel-shaped cloud extended from a thunder storm that reaches the ground from the sky.

Statement 2: Cyclones are caused by strong winds blowing around a central area having low atmospheric pressure.

(A) Statement 1 is true but statement 2 is false.
(B) Statement 2 is true but statement 1 is false.
(C) Both statement 1 and statement 2 are true but statement 2 is not the correct reason for statement 1.
(D) Both statement 1 and statement 2 are true and statement 2 is the correct reason for statement 1.

27. Which of the following is not a name for cyclone?
(A) Hurricane   (B) Willy-willy
(C) Temperate cyclone (D) Tornado

28. Sea and land breezes are caused due to __________.

(A) rains   (B) cyclones
(C) convection   (D) conduction

29. Following are precautions, one must take in case a storm is accompanied by lightning.
(i)   Do not take shelter under tree.
(ii) Do not take shelter under an umbrella with a metallic end.
(iii) Do not take shelter in open garages, storage sheds, etc.
(iv) Do not take shelter in a bus in the open.
Which one of these is not correct?
(A) (i)   (B) (ii)
(C) (iii)   (D) (iv)

30. A curtain is hanging at the entrance of a room. A long corridor runs at right angles to the door, that is parallel to the curtain. If a strong wind blows along the corridor, the curtain will
(A) get pushed inside the room
(B) get pushed outside the room
(C) get collected towards one end/ swirled
(D) remain unaffected

—————Darken Your Choice with HB Pencil —————

1.	Ⓐ Ⓑ Ⓒ Ⓓ	7.	Ⓐ Ⓑ Ⓒ Ⓓ	13.	Ⓐ Ⓑ Ⓒ Ⓓ	19	Ⓐ Ⓑ Ⓒ Ⓓ	25.	Ⓐ Ⓑ Ⓒ Ⓓ
2.	Ⓐ Ⓑ Ⓒ Ⓓ	8.	Ⓐ Ⓑ Ⓒ Ⓓ	14.	Ⓐ Ⓑ Ⓒ Ⓓ	20.	Ⓐ Ⓑ Ⓒ Ⓓ	26.	Ⓐ Ⓑ Ⓒ Ⓓ
3.	Ⓐ Ⓑ Ⓒ Ⓓ	9.	Ⓐ Ⓑ Ⓒ Ⓓ	15.	Ⓐ Ⓑ Ⓒ Ⓓ	21.	Ⓐ Ⓑ Ⓒ Ⓓ	27.	Ⓐ Ⓑ Ⓒ Ⓓ
4.	Ⓐ Ⓑ Ⓒ Ⓓ	10.	Ⓐ Ⓑ Ⓒ Ⓓ	16.	Ⓐ Ⓑ Ⓒ Ⓓ	22.	Ⓐ Ⓑ Ⓒ Ⓓ	28.	Ⓐ Ⓑ Ⓒ Ⓓ
5.	Ⓐ Ⓑ Ⓒ Ⓓ	11.	Ⓐ Ⓑ Ⓒ Ⓓ	17.	Ⓐ Ⓑ Ⓒ Ⓓ	23.	Ⓐ Ⓑ Ⓒ Ⓓ	29.	Ⓐ Ⓑ Ⓒ Ⓓ
6.	Ⓐ Ⓑ Ⓒ Ⓓ	12.	Ⓐ Ⓑ Ⓒ Ⓓ	18.	Ⓐ Ⓑ Ⓒ Ⓓ	24.	Ⓐ Ⓑ Ⓒ Ⓓ	30.	Ⓐ Ⓑ Ⓒ Ⓓ

NATURAL RESOURCES AND THEIR CONSERVATION

LEARNING OBJECTIVES

➤ The means of water management and its conservation
➤ The treatment of municipal waste water
➤ The importance of conservation of forest and trees

MULTIPLE CHOICE QUESTIONS

1. The solid part of the earth is called _______.
   - (A) hydrosphere
   - (B) lithosphere
   - (C) atmosphere
   - (D) all of these

2. Which of the following is mostly used as a drinking water source by us?
   - (A) sea water
   - (B) ground water
   - (C) glaciers
   - (D) none of these

3. Which of the following cause depletion in the water table of a place?
   - (A) making concrete roads and floors
   - (B) constructing factories and house
   - (C) deforestation
   - (D) all of these

4. Freshwater for human use on earth is _______.
   - (A) 0.3%
   - (B) 3%
   - (C) 0.03%
   - (D) 30%

5. The percentage of water in human body is _______.
   - (A) 80%
   - (B) 70%
   - (C) 60%
   - (D) 50%

6. Which of the following convert the dead plants and animals to humus?
   - (A) decomposers
   - (B) consumers
   - (C) chemicals
   - (D) scavengers

7. Plants and animals help in maintaining the balance of _______.
   - (A) water and minerals
   - (B) trees and animals
   - (C) oxygen and carbon dioxide
   - (D) green plants and plant eaters

8. Quinine is obtained from _______.
   - (A) bark of eucalyptus tree
   - (B) leaves of neem tree
   - (C) stem of poppy plants
   - (D) bark of cinchona tree

9. What is the major source of water in northernmost region of the world?
   - (A) glaciers
   - (B) rivers
   - (C) rainfall
   - (D) sea

10. Natural vegetation grows without _______.
    - (A) soil
    - (B) interference of human
    - (C) water
    - (D) plants

11. Which one of the following is not a forest product?
    - (A) soil
    - (B) lac
    - (C) fodder
    - (D) timber

12. The water table of a place ________.
  (A) changes from place to place
  (B) changes from time to time
  (C) goes down when rains are less
  (D) all of these
13. Which of the following is the most important factor in balancing the amount of fresh water on earth?
  (A) transpiration
  (B) WWTP
  (C) green house effect
  (D) water cycle
14. In the sewage treatment plant, which one of the following separates large solids such as leaves, rags, plastic etc?
  (A) aeration tank
  (B) strainers
  (C) sedimentation tank
  (D) all of these
15. In which of the following tanks aerobic bacteria breaks down organic waste present in sewage?
  (A) aeration tank
  (B) first sedimentation tank
  (C) second sedimentation tank
  (D) grit and sand removal tank
16. In which of the following activities, you need large quantity of water?
  (A) brushing your teeth
  (B) washing a pair of shirts
  (C) bathing under shower
  (D) bathing with bucket of water
17. A food chain will not begin in the absence of ________.
  (A) bacteria   (B) fungi
  (C) green plants   (D) animals
18. Which of the following bind the soil together?
  (A) rocks   (B) trees
  (C) layers of the soil (D) decomposers
19. Which of the following statements is not correct?
  (A) plants and animals in a forest are dependent on one another.
  (B) forest do not influence the climate and water cycle.
  (C) forests protects the soil from erosion.
  (D) soil helps the forests to grow and regenerate.
20. Which one of the following is the inorganic impurities present in sewage?
  (A) urine
  (B) animal dung
  (C) metals
  (D) vegetables wastes
21. The waste water coming from kitchen is called ________.
  (A) rainwater
  (B) municipal waste water
  (C) industrial waste water
  (D) both (B) and (C)
22. Which one of the following statements is correct?
  Statement 1: An underground pipe which carries away dirty drainage water is called sewer.
  Statement 2: The wastewater treatment plant is also called sewage treatment plant.
  (A) statement 1
  (B) statement 2
  (C) statements both are correct
  (D) statements both are incorrect
23. Which one of the following diseases is caused by microbes present in waste water?
  (A) cholera   (B) typhoid
  (C) dysentery   (D) all of these
24. Which one of the following is the organic impurities present in sewage?
  (A) plastics
  (B) vegetables wastes
  (C) metals
  (D) both (A) and (C)
25. Which one of the following nutrients are present in sewage?
  (A) phosphorus
  (B) chlorine
  (C) nitrogen
  (D) both (A) and (C)

26. **Statement 1:** The microorganisms like bacteria and fungi that convert dead and decaying animals and plants into humus are called decomposers.

    Statement 2: Sometimes the organic matters in the sewage break down by anaerobic bacteria in closed tank
    (A) Statement 1 is true but statement 2 is false.
    (B) Statement 2 is true but statement 1 is false.
    (C) Both statement 1 and statement 2 are true.
    (D) Both statement 1 and statement 2 are true and statement 2 is the correct reason for statement 1.

27. __________ is the flow of water molecules from the region of higher water potential to the region of lower water potential through a semi permeable membrane.
    (A) Osmosis
    (B) Diffusion
    (C) Both (A) and (B)
    (D) None

28. The large well like structure which was used in olden times for rainwater harvesting is called __________.
    (A) well
    (B) bawris
    (C) johad
    (D) check-dams

29. Which of the following doesn't show water shortage?
    (A) Taps running dry
    (B) Long queues for getting water
    (C) Marches and protests for demand of water
    (D) Three buckets of water per person per day

30. 'Every drop counts' is a slogan related to
    (A) counting of drops of any liquid
    (B) counting water drops
    (C) importance of water
    (D) importance of counting

Darken Your Choice with HB Pencil

	A B C D		A B C D		A B C D		A B C D		A B C D
1.	Ⓐ Ⓑ Ⓒ Ⓓ	7.	Ⓐ Ⓑ Ⓒ Ⓓ	13.	Ⓐ Ⓑ Ⓒ Ⓓ	19	Ⓐ Ⓑ Ⓒ Ⓓ	25.	Ⓐ Ⓑ Ⓒ Ⓓ
2.	Ⓐ Ⓑ Ⓒ Ⓓ	8.	Ⓐ Ⓑ Ⓒ Ⓓ	14.	Ⓐ Ⓑ Ⓒ Ⓓ	20.	Ⓐ Ⓑ Ⓒ Ⓓ	26.	Ⓐ Ⓑ Ⓒ Ⓓ
3.	Ⓐ Ⓑ Ⓒ Ⓓ	9.	Ⓐ Ⓑ Ⓒ Ⓓ	15.	Ⓐ Ⓑ Ⓒ Ⓓ	21.	Ⓐ Ⓑ Ⓒ Ⓓ	27.	Ⓐ Ⓑ Ⓒ Ⓓ
4.	Ⓐ Ⓑ Ⓒ Ⓓ	10.	Ⓐ Ⓑ Ⓒ Ⓓ	16.	Ⓐ Ⓑ Ⓒ Ⓓ	22.	Ⓐ Ⓑ Ⓒ Ⓓ	28.	Ⓐ Ⓑ Ⓒ Ⓓ
5.	Ⓐ Ⓑ Ⓒ Ⓓ	11.	Ⓐ Ⓑ Ⓒ Ⓓ	17.	Ⓐ Ⓑ Ⓒ Ⓓ	23.	Ⓐ Ⓑ Ⓒ Ⓓ	29.	Ⓐ Ⓑ Ⓒ Ⓓ
6.	Ⓐ Ⓑ Ⓒ Ⓓ	12.	Ⓐ Ⓑ Ⓒ Ⓓ	18.	Ⓐ Ⓑ Ⓒ Ⓓ	24.	Ⓐ Ⓑ Ⓒ Ⓓ	30.	Ⓐ Ⓑ Ⓒ Ⓓ

RESPIRATION IN ORGANISMS  9

LEARNING OBJECTIVES

- ➤ Respiration and analyze the need to respire
- ➤ The cellular respiration and its types – aerobic and anaerobic
- ➤ The process of respiration in human beings

MULTIPLE CHOICE QUESTIONS

1. The process by which gases are exchanged between the body and surrounding is called ________.
   - (A) breathing
   - (B) digestion
   - (C) excretion
   - (D) reproduction

2. Respiration is a/an ________ process.
   - (A) anabolic
   - (B) catabolic
   - (C) metabolic
   - (D) none

3. The food material used to release energy in body cells is ________.
   - (A) water
   - (B) oxygen
   - (C) glucose
   - (D) carbon dioxide

4. Plants exchange gases through ________.
   - (A) leaves
   - (B) stomata
   - (C) stem
   - (D) roots

5. Anaerobic respiration is also termed as ________.
   - (A) fermentation
   - (B) transportation
   - (C) imbibitions
   - (D) all of these

6. Fishes in aquarium are seen moving their mouth repeatedly because ________.
   - (A) they keep talking with it
   - (B) they keep eating with it
   - (C) they keep breathing with it
   - (D) they keep moving with it

7. In man, which of the following structures is analogous to the spiracles of cockroach?
   - (A) nostrils
   - (B) lungs
   - (C) bronchioles
   - (D) alveoli

8. To prevent the entry of food into the trachea, the opening is guarded by ________.
   - (A) glottis
   - (B) epiglottis
   - (C) soft palate
   - (D) hard palate

9. Respiratory membrane should be ________.
   - (A) permeable
   - (B) non-permeable
   - (C) semi-permeable
   - (D) none of these

10. The narrowest and most numerous tubes of lungs are termed as ________.
    - (A) alveoli
    - (B) bronchus
    - (C) bronchioles
    - (D) glottis

11. The bean-shaped cells of stomata are called __________.
    (A) peel cells
    (B) stomata
    (C) epithelial cells
    (D) guard cells

12. The number of guard cells forming a stomata is __________.
    (A) 2   (B) 3
    (C) 4   (D) 5

13. The actual site of gaseous exchange in respiratory system is __________.
    (A) trachea   (B) alveoli
    (C) bronchioles   (D) all of these

14. The trachea is prevented from collapsing by __________.
    (A) bony rings
    (B) chitinous rings
    (C) complete cartilaginous rings
    (D) incomplete cartilaginous rings

15. In cockroach the tracheal system opens in the outside through __________.
    (A) anus   (B) mouth
    (C) stigmata   (D) dorsal pores

16. Which of the following diagram correctly illustrates the passage of oxygen in the respiratory system?
    (A) Nose → lungs → wind pipe → blood
    (B) Nose → blood → wind pipe → lungs
    (C) Nose → wind pipe → lungs → blood
    (D) Nose → blood → lungs → wind pipe

17. Gills are used for __________.
    (A) pulmonary respiration
    (B) aquatic respiration
    (C) terrestrial respiration
    (D) all types of respiration

18. The short tube leading from the nose is __________.
    (A) alveoli   (B) trachea
    (C) bronchi   (D) pharynx

19. Air goes from pharynx to __________.
    (A) trachea   (B) bronchi
    (C) bronchus   (D) bronchiole

20. Lactic acid accumulation leads to __________.
    (A) kidney fatigue
    (B) muscle fatigue
    (C) liver fatigue
    (D) all of these

21. In most unicellular organisms __________.
    (A) oxygen is absorbed through lungs
    (B) oxygen is absorbed by spiracles
    (C) oxygen is diffused into cell
    (D) oxygen is absorbed through alveoli

22. Alcohol is the product of __________.
    (A) Aerobic respiration
    (B) Anaerobic respiration
    (C) fermentation
    (D) both (B) & (C)

23. Which of the following forms the floor of the chest cavity?
    (A) pleura   (B) lungs
    (C) diaphragm   (D) membrane

24. In the given figure, diaphragm is represented by __________.

    (A) P   (B) Q
    (C) R   (D) S

25. What happens to the lime water, when we exhale air into it?
    (A) turns blue
    (B) turns to milky
    (C) remains same
    (D) become colourless

26. Which of the following animals breathe through their skin and lungs?
    (A) fish   (B) frog
    (C) snake   (D) earthworm

27. In fishes gills are the respiratory organs, gills are projections of which of the following parts?
    (A) skin
    (B) nostril
    (C) alimentary canal
    (D) none of these

28. Which of the following statements is not correct?
    (A) taking in of oxygen is inhalation
    (B) taking in of carbon dioxide is inhalation
    (C) giving out of carbon dioxide is exhalation
    (D) number of inhalation and exhalation in one minute is known as breathing rate

29. The function of hair follicles inside the nose is __________.
    (A) to moisten the air
    (B) to detect the presence of oxygen in air.
    (C) to trap germs and dust particles in the air
    (D) to control the amount of air being inhaled.

30. In man, nasal and oral cavities are separated by __________.
    (A) palate
    (B) diaphragm
    (C) both (A) and (B)
    (D) none

HOTS (ACHIEVERS SECTION)

Directions (31–32): Study the diagram for internal structure of heart, given below and answer the following questions.

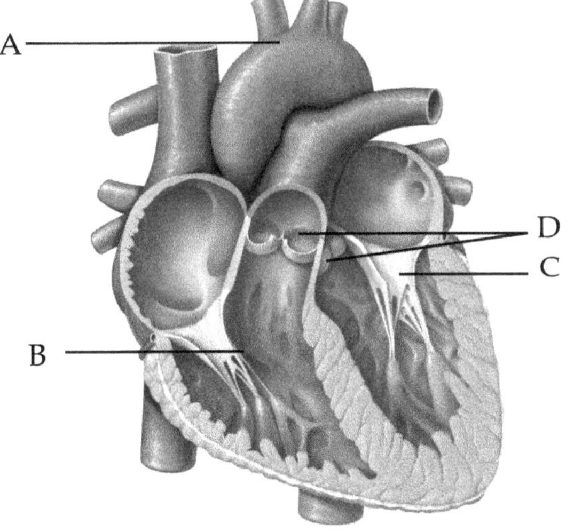

31. Which part of human heart guards the opening of right atrium into right ventricle?
    (A) A   (B) B
    (C) C   (D) D

32. Which of the following guards the opening of left atrium into left ventricle?
    (A) A
    (B) B
    (C) C
    (D) D

33. The actual site of gaseous exchange in respiratory system is __________.
    (A) trachea
    (B) bronchioles
    (C) wind pipe
    (D) alveoli

34. Sometimes when we do heavy exercise, anaerobic respiration takes place in our muscle cells. What is produced during this process?
   (A) Alcohol and lactic acid
   (B) Alcohol and CO_2
   (C) Lactic acid and CO_2
   (D) Lactic acid only

35. Yeast is used in wine and beer industries because it respires
   (A) aerobically producing oxygen
   (B) aerobically producing alcohol
   (C) anaerobically producing ethanol and CO_2
   (D) anaerobically producing CO_2

1.	A B C D	8.	A B C D	15.	A B C D	22	A B C D	29.	A B C D
2.	A B C D	9.	A B C D	16.	A B C D	23.	A B C D	30.	A B C D
3.	A B C D	10.	A B C D	17.	A B C D	24.	A B C D	31.	A B C D
4.	A B C D	11.	A B C D	18.	A B C D	25.	A B C D	32.	A B C D
5.	A B C D	12.	A B C D	19.	A B C D	26.	A B C D	33.	A B C D
6.	A B C D	13.	A B C D	20.	A B C D	27.	A B C D	34.	A B C D
7.	A B C D	14.	A B C D	21.	A B C D	28.	A B C D	35.	A B C D

TRANSPORTATION AND EXCRETION

LEARNING OBJECTIVES

➤ Circulatory system and its components
➤ Blood vessels – arteries, veins and capillaries
➤ Transportation in plants through vascular bundles xylem and phloem

MULTIPLE CHOICE QUESTIONS

1. Which organ of the circulatory system pump blood?
   (A) kidneys   (B) heart
   (C) lungs   (D) blood

2. The solution of minerals, water, food and gases that is circulated through xylem and phloem is called _______.
   (A) sol   (B) sap
   (C) protoplasm   (D) cytoplasm

3. The solution of water and minerals absorbed by the roots move upwards to the other parts of the plant through _______.
   (A) xylem   (B) phloem
   (C) spiracles   (D) blood vessels

4. Which material is not a waste in man?
   (A) Glucose   (B) urea
   (C) carbon dioxide   (D) water

5. Kidneys are located in _______.
   (A) the chest
   (B) the abdomen
   (C) the hands
   (D) the left side of the body

6. The ultimate cause of the movement of water against gravity in a tree is _______.
   (A) osmosis
   (B) imbibition
   (C) transpiration
   (D) photosynthesis

7. Which of the following has no muscular walls?
   (A) capillary   (B) vein
   (C) artery   (D) arteriole

8. Transpiration is _______.
   (A) the movement of sap upward in a plant against the force of gravity.
   (B) the absorption of waste materials from the blood by nephrons.
   (C) the absorption of water and minerals by the roots of a plant.
   (D) the loss of water and waste material through stomata and lenticels.

9. Glucose solution when treated with Benedict's solution and heated turns _______.
   (A) pink   (B) red
   (C) yellow   (D) blue

10. The upper chambers of the heart are called _______.
    (A) auricles   (B) ventricles
    (C) spiracles   (D) tentacles

11. The lower chambers of the heart are called _______.
    (A) auricles   (B) ventricles
    (C) spiracles   (D) tentacles

12. _______ pump deoxygenated blood to the lungs.
    (A) right auricle   (B) left auricle
    (C) right ventricle   (D) left ventricle

13. _______ receives oxygenated blood from the lungs.
    (A) left auricle   (B) right auricle
    (C) left ventricle   (D) right ventricle

14. Which of the following statements is false?
    (A) Oxygenated blood is pumped to all other parts of the body from left ventricle.
    (B) Blood from the right side of the heart enters into left side through right auricle and left auricle.
    (C) Gaseous exchange in the alveoli happens through capillaries.
    (D) Lungs oxygenate the deoxygenated blood.

15. Root hair of root of a plant absorbs _______.
    (A) water   (B) oxygen
    (C) salts   (D) all of these

16. The droplets of water arranged at the edges of leaves of roses in the morning are _______.
    (A) water transpired from the stomata and lenticels.
    (B) water drops condensed from the atmosphere during night at low temperatures.
    (C) water produced on the leaves from the reaction of hydrogen and atmospheric oxygen.
    (D) none of these

17. Plant cells store waste materials in _______.
    (A) vacuoles   (B) old leaves
    (C) both (A) and (B) (D) none of these

18. When the muscles of the heart contract _______.
    (A) blood flows from the lungs into the left auricle
    (B) blood is pumped into the right auricle from all over the body
    (C) blood is pumped from the right ventricle into the lungs
    (D) none of these

19. When the muscles of the heart relax _______.
    (A) blood is pumped into the right auricle from all over the body
    (B) blood flows from lungs into the left auricle
    (C) both (A) and (B)
    (D) blood flows from the left ventricle to the rest of the body.

20. Blood from the left ventricle is pumped to _______.
    (A) left auricle
    (B) right auricle
    (C) all parts of the body
    (D) lungs

21. Match the following .
    i.   Kidneys   A. air
    ii. Heart   B. food
    iii. Lungs   C. blood
    iv. Stomach   D. wastes
    (A) i - A, ii - C, iii - D, iv - B
    (B) i - D, ii - C, iii - B, iv - A
    (C) i - C, ii - D, iii - B, iv - A
    (D) i - D, ii - C, iii - A, iv - B

22. In potato experiment, sugar level inside potato is increased due to _______.
    (A) sugar solution absorbs water
    (B) movement of water from outside to inside
    (C) potato containing stored water
    (D) there is no change

23. _______ is the flow of water molecules from the region of higher water pressure to the region of lower water pressure through a semipermeable membrane.

(A) diffusion
(B) transpiration
(C) osmosis
(D) none of these

24. _______ animals excrete ammonia in gaseous form.
(A) land animals
(B) desert animals
(C) aerial animals
(D) aquatic animals

25. Human heart represents _______.
(A) double circulation
(B) pulmonary circulation
(C) systemic circulation
(D) none of these

26. Which among the following contain haemoglobin?
(A) Red blood cells
(B) White blood cells
(C) Both (A) and (B)
(D) None of these

27. They are pipe-like consisting of a group of specialised cells. They transport substances and form a two-way traffic in plants. Which of the following terms qualifies for the features mentioned above?
(A) Xylem tissue
(B) Vascular tissue
(C) Root hairs
(D) Phloem tissue

28. The absorption of nutrients and exchange of respiratory gases between blood and tissues takes place in
(A) veins   (B) arteries
(C) heart   (D) capillaries

29. In which of the following parts of human body are sweat glands absent?
(A) Scalp   (B) Armpits
(C) Lips   (D) Palms

30. In a tall tree which force is responsible for pulling water and minerals from the soil?
(A) Gravitational force
(B) Transportation force
(C) Suction force
(D) Conduction force

Darken Your Choice with HB Pencil

1.	(A) (B) (C) (D)	7.	(A) (B) (C) (D)	13.	(A) (B) (C) (D)	19	(A) (B) (C) (D)	25.	(A) (B) (C) (D)
2.	(A) (B) (C) (D)	8.	(A) (B) (C) (D)	14.	(A) (B) (C) (D)	20.	(A) (B) (C) (D)	26.	(A) (B) (C) (D)
3.	(A) (B) (C) (D)	9.	(A) (B) (C) (D)	15.	(A) (B) (C) (D)	21.	(A) (B) (C) (D)	27.	(A) (B) (C) (D)
4.	(A) (B) (C) (D)	10.	(A) (B) (C) (D)	16.	(A) (B) (C) (D)	22.	(A) (B) (C) (D)	28.	(A) (B) (C) (D)
5.	(A) (B) (C) (D)	11.	(A) (B) (C) (D)	17.	(A) (B) (C) (D)	23.	(A) (B) (C) (D)	29.	(A) (B) (C) (D)
6.	(A) (B) (C) (D)	12.	(A) (B) (C) (D)	18.	(A) (B) (C) (D)	24.	(A) (B) (C) (D)	30.	(A) (B) (C) (D)

REPRODUCTION IN PLANTS 

LEARNING OBJECTIVES

➤ The various modes of reproduction
➤ The methods of vegetative propagation
➤ Sexual reproduction, pollination and fertilization

MULTIPLE CHOICE QUESTIONS

1. In asexual reproduction ———·
   (A) one parent is involved
   (B) both parents are involved
   (C) no parent is involved
   (D) all of these

2. Vegetative reproduction is ———·
   (A) a sexual reproduction
   (B) an asexual reproduction
   (C) a pollination
   (D) an antisexual reproduction

3. Spores are ———·
   (A) outgrowths from parent organism.
   (B) buds formed in long chains.
   (C) tiny cells protected by thick walls to survive unfavourable conditions.
   (D) new organisms growing from tuberous roots.

4. Yeast cells reproduce by ———·
   (A) fission   (B) spirulation
   (C) budding   (D) all of these

5. Onion is a ———·
   (A) bulb   (B) fruit
   (C) vegetable   (D) none of these

6. Pollen grains are produced from ———·
   (A) stigma   (B) ovary
   (C) style   (D) none of these

7. Sweet potatoes reproduce from ———·
   (A) modified roots
   (B) modified leaves
   (C) modified stem
   (D) modified flowers

8. Ferns reproduce through ———·
   (A) binary fission
   (B) gladioli
   (C) spore formation
   (D) regeneration

9. Mushrooms reproduce through ———·
   (A) modified stems
   (B) spores
   (C) spore formation
   (D) buds on the leaf margin

10. Bryophyllum grows from ———·
    (A) bulbs of the modified stems.
    (B) eyes on the tuberous roots.
    (C) buds on the modified leaves.
    (D) outgrowths from the modified roots.

11. The male gamete in plants is called ———·
    (A) testes   (B) semen
    (C) pollengrain   (D) penis

12. The female gamete in plants is called ________.
   (A) vagina   (B) ovary
   (C) uterus   (D) egg
13. Male part of a flower is called ________.
   (A) egg   (B) pollen tube
   (C) stamen   (D) stigma
14. The long stalk in the stamen is called ________.
   (A) anther   (B) filament
   (C) pollen tube   (D) style
15. Female part of the flower is called ________.
   (A) pistil   (B) corolla
   (C) stamen   (D) pollen tube
16. When you add yeast to dough, it arises because ________.
   (A) of the bulk of the new yeast cells
   (B) yeast cells reproduce by budding
   (C) budding yeast cells from colonies
   (D) the rapidly reproducing yeast cells release carbon dioxide due to anaerobic respiration.
17. Which of the following constitute a pistil?
   (A) pollen sac, style and ovule
   (B) stigma, style and ovary
   (C) stigma, stamen and ovary
   (D) stigma, anther and ovary
18. Flowers which have stamens and pistils are called ________.
   (A) complete flowers
   (B) incomplete flowers
   (C) unisexual flowers
   (D) homosexual flowers
19. Female gametes are present in ________.
   (A) stigma   (B) ovary
   (C) pollen tube   (D) anther
20. Male gametes are present in ________.
   (A) style   (B) filament
   (C) anther   (D) stigma
21. Style belongs to ________.
   (A) pistil   (B) stamen
   (C) both   (D) none of these

22. Scattering of seeds over a wide area is called ________.
   (A) fertilization   (B) dispersal
   (C) germination   (D) pollination
23. The seeds of ______ fruit are dry and dispersed by explosion due to the touch of our hands.
   (A) cucumber   (B) xanthium
   (C) balsam   (D) calotropis
24. The seed with thick fibrous outer covering is ________.
   (A) lime   (B) coconut
   (C) papaya   (D) neem
25. The sequence of life cycle of a plant is ________.
   (A) seed, seedling, plant, sapling
   (B) sapling, seedling, seed, plant
   (C) seed, seedling, sapling, plant
   (D) seedling, seed, plant, sapling
26. Seeds with hooks are dispersed by ________.
   (A) wind
   (B) animals
   (C) water
   (D) explosion mechanism
27. If you cut an ovary of mustard flower, you will see ________.
   (A) fruits   (B) stem
   (C) flowers   (D) ovules
28. Match the columns ________.

Column A	Column B
i. Amoeba	A. Spore formation
ii. Plasmodium	B. Binary fission
iii. Yeast	C. Vegetative propagation
iv. Mucor	D. Budding
v. Potato	E. Multiple fission

   (A) i - B, ii - E, iii - D, iv - A, v - C
   (B) i - C, ii - D, iii - B, iv - C, v - A
   (C) i - D, ii - A, iii - E, iv - B, v - C
   (D) i - E, ii - C, iii - A, iv - B, v - D

29. _______ develops into embryo.
   (A) chaloza (B) zygote
   (C) pollen grain (D) micropyle

30. Rose and champa reproduces by ________.
   (A) grafting (B) root cutting
   (C) layering (D) stem cutting

HOTS (ACHIEVERS SECTION)

31. Which of these is/are correct advantage of vegetative propagation?
   (i) Plants produced by the method of vegetative propagation mature earlier than those plants which are produced by seeds.
   (ii) Plants grown by vegetative propagation methods need less attention in their early stages of growth than the plants grown from seeds.
   (A) Only (i)
   (B) Only (ii)
   (C) Both (i) and (ii)
   (D) Neither (i) or (ii)

32. The 'eye' of the potato plant is what?
   (A) The root is to any plant
   (B) The bud is to a flower
   (C) The bud is to Bryophyllum leaf
   (D) The anther is to stamen

33. Seeds of drumstick and maple are carried to long distances by wind because they possess.
   (A) Winged seeds
   (B) Large and hairy seeds
   (C) Long and ridged fruits
   (D) Spiny seeds

34. Lila observed that a pond with clear water was covered up with a green algae within a week. By which method of reproduction did the algae spread so rapidly?
   (A) Budding
   (B) Sexual reproduction
   (C) Fragmentation
   (D) Pollination

35. Which of the following parts of asexual reproduction?
   (i) Flower (ii) Seed
   (iii) Fruit (iv) Branch
   Choose the correct answer from below
   (A) (i) and (ii)
   (B) (i), (ii) and (iii)
   (C) (iii) and (iv)
   (D) (ii), (iii) and (iv)

—Darken Your Choice with HB Pencil—

1.	Ⓐ Ⓑ Ⓒ Ⓓ	8.	Ⓐ Ⓑ Ⓒ Ⓓ	15.	Ⓐ Ⓑ Ⓒ Ⓓ	22	Ⓐ Ⓑ Ⓒ Ⓓ	29.	Ⓐ Ⓑ Ⓒ Ⓓ
2.	Ⓐ Ⓑ Ⓒ Ⓓ	9.	Ⓐ Ⓑ Ⓒ Ⓓ	16.	Ⓐ Ⓑ Ⓒ Ⓓ	23.	Ⓐ Ⓑ Ⓒ Ⓓ	30.	Ⓐ Ⓑ Ⓒ Ⓓ
3.	Ⓐ Ⓑ Ⓒ Ⓓ	10.	Ⓐ Ⓑ Ⓒ Ⓓ	17.	Ⓐ Ⓑ Ⓒ Ⓓ	24.	Ⓐ Ⓑ Ⓒ Ⓓ	31.	Ⓐ Ⓑ Ⓒ Ⓓ
4.	Ⓐ Ⓑ Ⓒ Ⓓ	11.	Ⓐ Ⓑ Ⓒ Ⓓ	18.	Ⓐ Ⓑ Ⓒ Ⓓ	25.	Ⓐ Ⓑ Ⓒ Ⓓ	32.	Ⓐ Ⓑ Ⓒ Ⓓ
5.	Ⓐ Ⓑ Ⓒ Ⓓ	12.	Ⓐ Ⓑ Ⓒ Ⓓ	19.	Ⓐ Ⓑ Ⓒ Ⓓ	26.	Ⓐ Ⓑ Ⓒ Ⓓ	33.	Ⓐ Ⓑ Ⓒ Ⓓ
6.	Ⓐ Ⓑ Ⓒ Ⓓ	13.	Ⓐ Ⓑ Ⓒ Ⓓ	20.	Ⓐ Ⓑ Ⓒ Ⓓ	27.	Ⓐ Ⓑ Ⓒ Ⓓ	34.	Ⓐ Ⓑ Ⓒ Ⓓ
7.	Ⓐ Ⓑ Ⓒ Ⓓ	14.	Ⓐ Ⓑ Ⓒ Ⓓ	21.	Ⓐ Ⓑ Ⓒ Ⓓ	28.	Ⓐ Ⓑ Ⓒ Ⓓ	35.	Ⓐ Ⓑ Ⓒ Ⓓ

MOTION AND TIME

LEARNING OBJECTIVES

- ➤ Motion
- ➤ Uniform and non-uniform motion
- ➤ A pendulum
- ➤ Distance and displacement
- ➤ A distance-time graph
- ➤ Various devices used for measuring time

MULTIPLE CHOICE QUESTIONS

1. If a body moves in a circle, it starts from point A and after completing the circle comes back to A; the displacement of such body is ______.
   (A) equal to the diameter of circle
   (B) equal to the circumference of circle
   (C) zero
   (D) none of these

2. The CGS unit of speed is __________.
   (A) cm/g   (B) cm/s
   (C) m/s   (D) m/g

3. One mean solar day is equal to how many seconds?
   (A) 80,406   (B) 80,640
   (C) 86,400   (D) 84,600

4. Which of the following graphs does not represent constant speed?

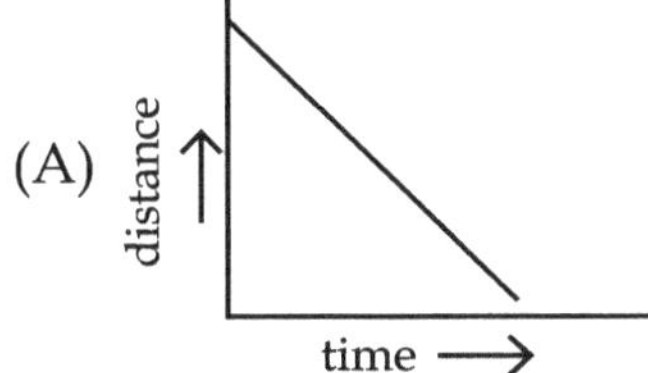
(A)

(B)

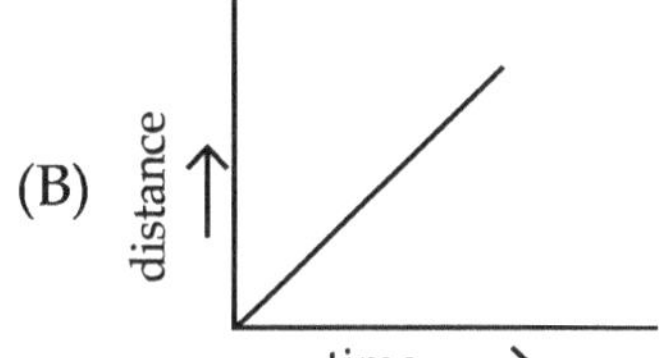

(C)

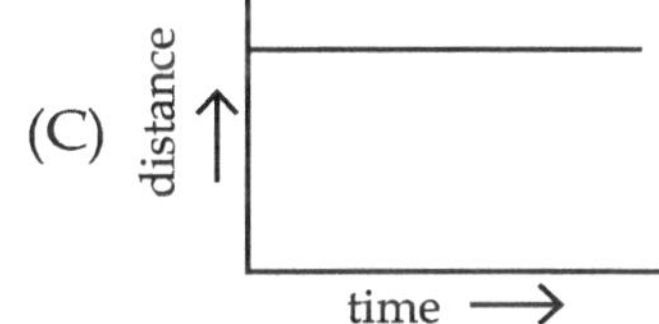

(D)

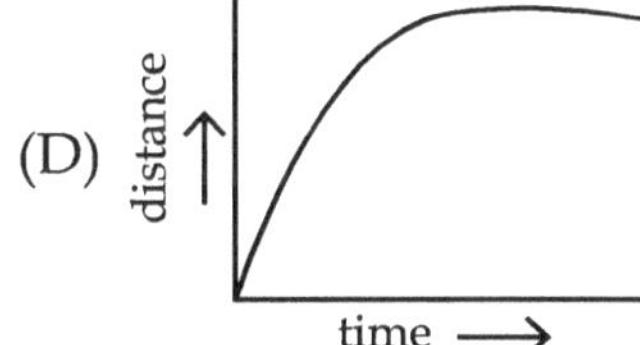

5. Which of the following is in uniform motion?
   (A) a swinging pendulum
   (B) the rotation of earth
   (C) a bullet travelling with a constant speed in a straight line
   (D) all of those

6. Which of the following does not show oscillatory motion?
   (A) swing   (B) fan
   (C) see-saw   (D) pendulum
7. A jet is moving with a speed of 180 km/h. What is its speed in m/s?
   (A) 50 m/s   (B) 10 m/s
   (C) 500 m/s   (D) 100 m/s
8. Which of the following is the fastest?
   (A) wind   (B) light
   (C) sound   (D) cheetah
9. Which of the following is matched incorrectly?
   (A) Anemometer : wind speed
   (B) Stopwatch   : time
   (C) Odometer   : odour
   (D) Speedometer : speed
10. Distance travelled will be equal to the displacement if __________.
   (A) object is moving along straight line in forward direction.
   (B) object is moving in different directions.
   (C) object is moving from one point to other along any path.
   (D) not possible in any condition.
11. The area of the shaded portion in the graph shown below represents?

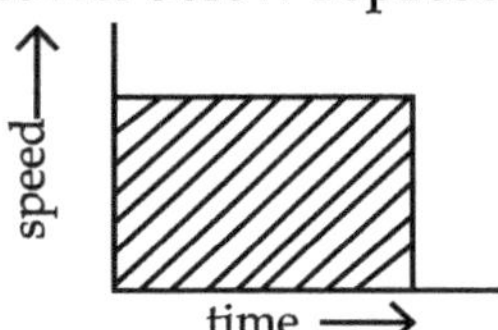

   (A) distance   (B) speed
   (C) time   (D) none of these
12. The following graph shows the motion of four runners. P, Q, R and S in a 5 km marathon. Whose motion is the fastest?

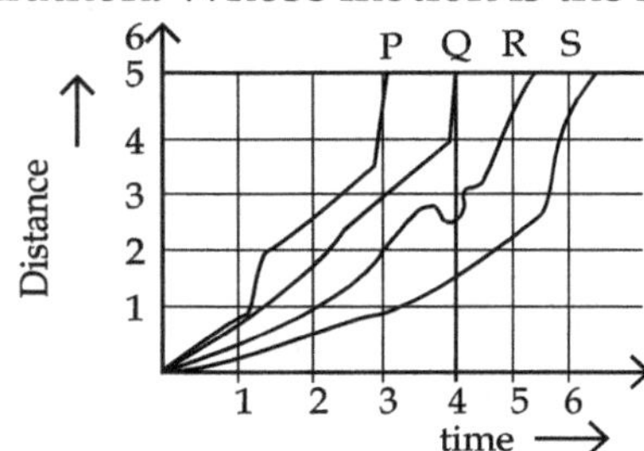

13. With what speed should a car travel so that it can cover a distance of 5 km in 5 min?
   (A) 1 km/h
   (B) 5 km/h
   (C) 12 km/h
   (D) 60 km/h
14. All of the following are units time except __________.
   (A) years
   (B) light years
   (C) seconds
   (D) months
15. Study the graph given below. How is the speed of the moving body?

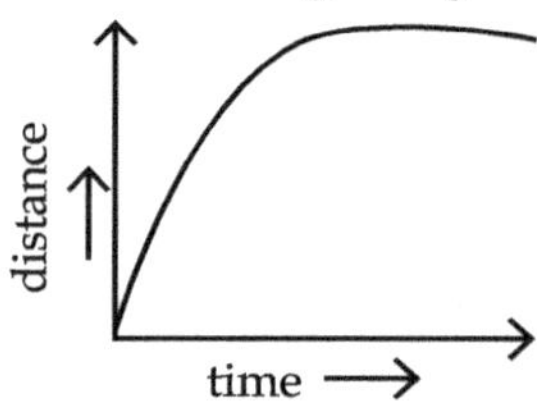

   (A) It goes on increasing
   (B) It increases and then becomes constant but not zero
   (C) First it decreases and then becomes zero
   (D) It decreases and then becomes constant but not zero
16. Which of the following shows a motion in a straight line?
   (A) apple falling from the tree
   (B) tree swaying
   (C) child on a merry-go-round
   (D) none of these
17. Riaz takes 20 minutes to travel to his schools with a speed of 3 m/s. How far is the school?
   (A) 2 km   (B) 3.2 km
   (C) 3.6 km   (D) 4.1 km

18. Which of the following graph represents the movement of a car that is slowing down and comes to a complete stop?

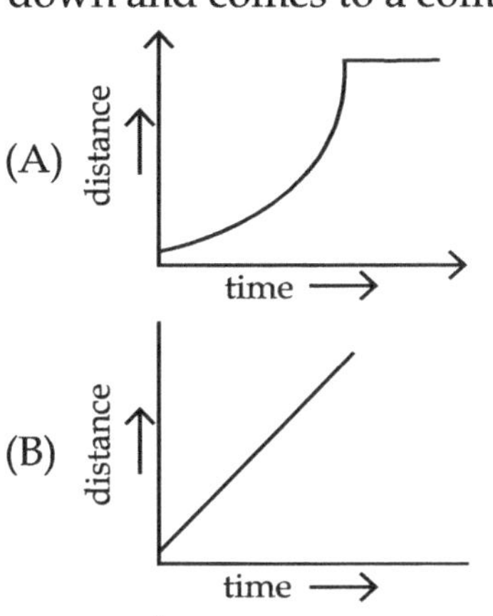

(A)

(B)

(C)

(D)

19. Change the speed 20 m/s to km/hr ____.
   (A) 27 km/hr   (B) 28 km/hr
   (C) 72 km/hr   (D) 73 km/hr

20. Which of the following is a disadvantage of Sundial?
   (A) It's difficult to build a Sundial
   (B) It is difficult to predict time with a Sundial
   (C) It occupies a large area
   (D) It does not work after sunset or on a cloudy day

21. Study the diagram given below and answer the question.

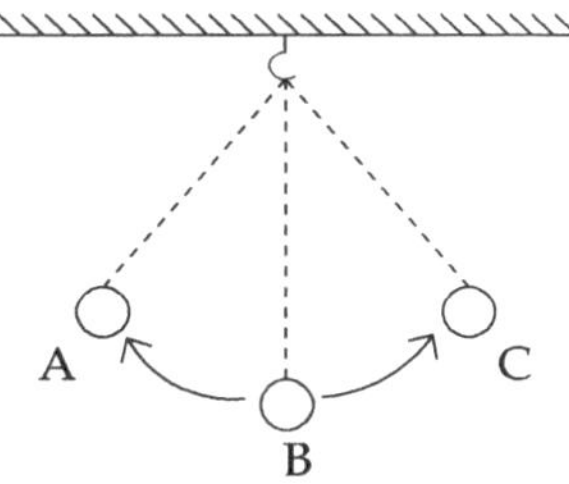

Simple Pendulum

Which of the given position of the bob will give the amplitude of the pendulum?
   (A) At A   (B) At B
   (C) At C   (D) Both A and B

22. Which of the following graphs does not represent uniform speed ?

(A)

(B)

(C)

(D)

23. With what speed should a car travel so that it can cover a distance of 8 km. in 15 minutes?
   (A) 32 km/h   (B) 60 km/h
   (C) 16 km/h   (D) 7.5 km/h

24. An odometer is used to measure _______.
   (A) speed   (B) time
   (C) distance   (D) temperature

25. An object may be in the rest as well as in the motion in the same time. Which one of the following is correct explanation for the above statement?
   (A) Rest and motion are defined on basis of position of an object. So a body may be in rest and in the motion at the same time.
   (B) Object is in rest or in motion depends on the reference point. An object may be in motion with respect to a reference point and at same time the object may be in rest with respect to another reference point.
   (C) Rotatory motion justifies the above statement. In the rotatory motion, object rotates around a fixed axis and does not cover distance. Therefore, object is in motion and in the rest at the same time.
   (D) No, it is not possible that an object is in the motion and in the rest as well.

1.	A B C D	6.	A B C D	11.	A B C D	16	A B C D	21.	A B C D
2.	A B C D	7.	A B C D	12.	A B C D	17.	A B C D	22.	A B C D
3.	A B C D	8.	A B C D	13.	A B C D	18.	A B C D	23.	A B C D
4.	A B C D	9.	A B C D	14.	A B C D	19.	A B C D	24.	A B C D
5.	A B C D	10.	A B C D	15.	A B C D	20.	A B C D	25.	A B C D

ELECTRIC CURRENT AND ITS EFFECTS

LEARNING OBJECTIVES

➤ The heating effect of electric current
➤ Magnetic effects of current
➤ The working of an electromagnet and electric bell

MULTIPLE CHOICE QUESTIONS

1. The shorter, thicker vertical line in the symbol of a cell represents _________.
   (A) the direction of current
   (B) the negative terminal
   (C) the positive terminal
   (D) all of these

2. 'The wire of more resistance produces more amount of heat energy'. Is the statement true?
   (A) Yes
   (B) No
   (C) resistance has nothing to do with heat
   (D) none of these

3. An electric circuit is a path along which an electric current may flow. The main components of an electric circuit are _________.
   (A) source of energy
   (B) output device
   (C) connecting wire and key
   (D) all of these

4. Which of the following is an electrical conductor?
   (A) cork
   (B) silver
   (C) wood
   (D) silver-coloured plastic

5. In which circuit will the bulb or bulbs glow the brightest?
   (A) A simple circuit with one bulb and one cell.
   (B) A simple circuit with one bulb and two cells.
   (C) A simple circuit with two bulbs and one cell.
   (D) A simple circuit with two bulbs and two cell.

6. A material that does not allow electricity to flow through it is called a/an _________.
   (A) electrical appliance
   (B) key
   (C) electrical insulator
   (D) electrical conductor

7. Why is electrical wiring usually covered with a layer of plastic?
   (A) To make it safe
   (B) To make it strong
   (C) To help electricity flow in it
   (D) To make it beautiful

8. The heating element in heater, toaster etc. is made of an alloy of __________.
   (A) brass
   (B) steel
   (C) nichrome
   (D) tungsten

9. The bulb in the circuit given here does not glow. Which labeled part is responsible for this?

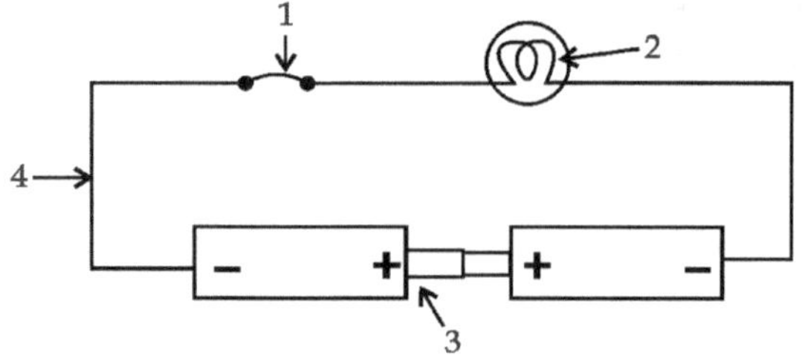

   (A) 1
   (B) 2
   (C) 3
   (D) 4

10. Electromagnetic induction was first discovered by __________.
    (A) Michael Faraday
    (B) Hans Christian Oersted
    (C) William Sturgeon
    (D) Benjamin Frankin

11. The requirement of a fuse is that it must be a/an __________.
    (A) insulator with low melting point
    (B) insulator with high boiling point
    (C) conductor with low melting point
    (D) conductor with high melting point

12. Electric generators are based on the principle of __________.
    (A) electromagnets
    (B) electromagnetic induction
    (C) electricity
    (D) none

13. Which of the following statements regarding an electromagnet is not true?
    (A) It is used in fans and radio
    (B) It works only in the presence of electricity
    (C) It is a permanent magnet
    (D) Insulated wire is wound around it

14. In which of the following arrangements, bulb will be able to glow?

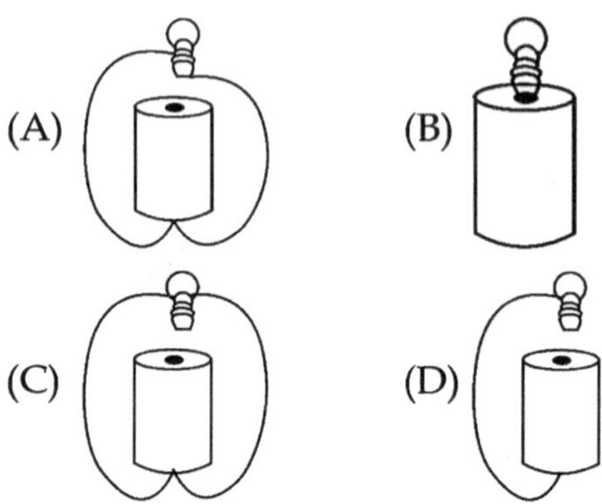

15. Compass needle shows deflection when __________.
    (A) brought near magnet
    (B) brought near current carrying wire
    (C) both are true
    (D) both are false

16. Which of following is the symbol for a bulb?
    (A) —⋀⋀⋀—
    (B) —(·)—
    (C) ___Ω___
    (D) —⊣⊢—

17. Rizvi has connected two bulbs across two cells in a simple circuit. How can he make the bulbs dimmer?
    (A) Replace one of the cells with a cork.
    (B) replace one of the bulbs with a cork.
    (C) replace one of the cells with a wire.
    (D) replace one of the bulbs with a wire.

18. Why is electrical wiring usually made from copper and not silver?
    (A) copper is a better conductor
    (B) copper is a better insulator
    (C) copper is less expensive
    (D) copper is non magnetic

19. Study the circuit shown here; which switch, if opened, will cause the light bulb to stop glowing?

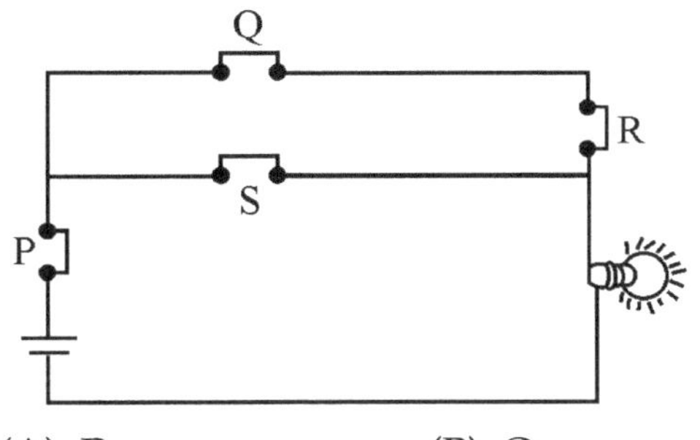

(A) P   (B) Q

(C) R   (D) none of these

20. Which of the following instruments is used to check whether electricity is flowing through a substance or not?

    (A) ammeter   (B) voltmeter

    (C) cell   (D) tester

21. When a current is drawn from the cell, circuit is said to be ____________.

    (A) closed circuit

    (B) open circuit

    (C) incomplete circuit

    (D) none of these

22. In electromagnetic induction, the magnitude of current can be increased when ____________.

    (A) the strength of the magnet increases

    (B) speed of movement of coil or magnet increases

    (C) a number of loops of wire increase

    (D) all of these

23. Pooja makes a simple circuit with one bulb and five cells. The bulb lights for an instant and then goes out. Why?

    (A) the wires melted in the heat

    (B) too much electricity passed through the bulb filament

    (C) electricity could not flow through the circuit

    (D) all of these

24. When the two terminals of a cell are connected directly with a wire, then ____________.

    (A) no current flows

    (B) the chemicals gets used up very fast

    (C) more electrical energy is stored in the cell

    (D) the cell explodes

25. Look at the following figure and find the position of the image

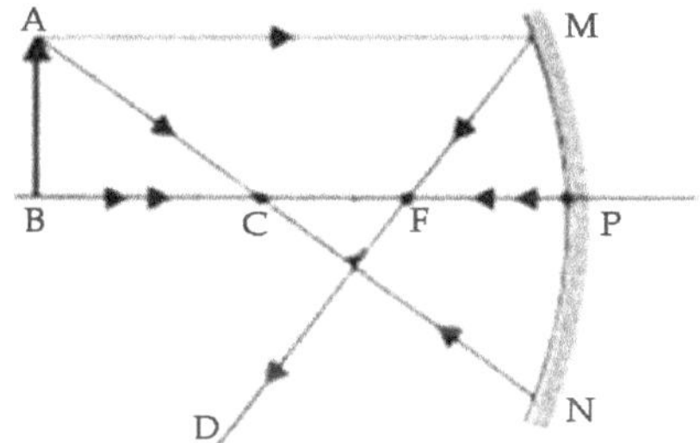

    (A) At pole

    (B) At focus

    (C) Between focus and centre of curvature

    (D) Beyond centre of curvature

HOTS (ACHIEVERS SECTION)

26. **Statement 1:** Mostly metals like copper, iron and aluminium are used to make the solar heating pipes and boilers in chemical and textile industries.

    Statement 2: Copper, iron and aluminium are good conductor of electricity.

    (A) Statement 1 is true but statement 2 is false.

    (B) Statement 2 is true but statement 1 is false.

    (C) Both statement 1 and statement 2 are true but statement 2 is not the correct reason for statement 1.

    (D) Both statement 1 and statement 2 are true and statement 2 is the correct reason for statement 1.

27. An electric heater is used in kitchens to cook food, it converts electrical energy to ________.
   (A) heat energy
   (B) light energy
   (C) both (A) and (B)
   (B) chemical energy

28. Which of the following precautions need not be taken while using electric gadgets/appliances/circuit?
   (A) We should never touch a lighted electric bulb connected to the mains.
   (B) We should never do experiment with the electric supply from the mains or a generator or an inverter.
   (C) We should never use just any wire or strip of metal in place of a fuse.
   (D) We should never turn the switch in ON position.

29. When a switch is in OFF position:
   (i) circuit starting from the positive terminal of the cell stops at the switch
   (ii) circuit is open
   (iii) no current flows through it
   (iv) current flows after sometime

Choose the combination of correct answer from the following.
   (A) All are correct
   (B) (ii) and (iii) are correct
   (C) Only (iv) is correct
   (D) (i) and (ii) are correct

30. When an electric current flows through a copper wire AB as shown in figure, the wire

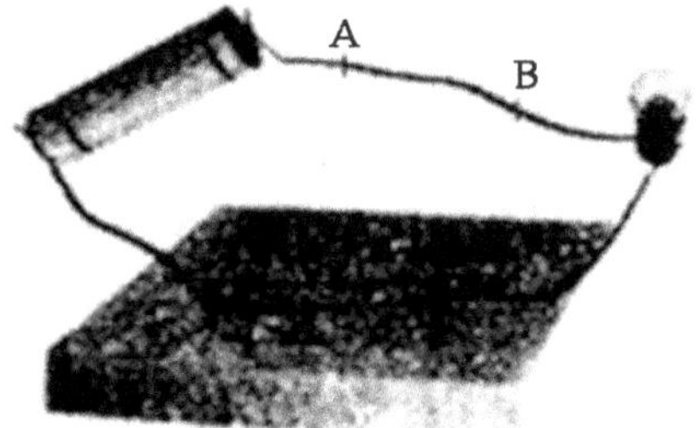

   (A) deflects a magnetic needle placed near it
   (B) becomes red hot
   (C) gives electric shock
   (D) behaves like a fuse

―――Darken Your Choice with HB Pencil―――

1.	Ⓐ Ⓑ Ⓒ Ⓓ	7.	Ⓐ Ⓑ Ⓒ Ⓓ	13.	Ⓐ Ⓑ Ⓒ Ⓓ	19	Ⓐ Ⓑ Ⓒ Ⓓ	25.	Ⓐ Ⓑ Ⓒ Ⓓ
2.	Ⓐ Ⓑ Ⓒ Ⓓ	8.	Ⓐ Ⓑ Ⓒ Ⓓ	14.	Ⓐ Ⓑ Ⓒ Ⓓ	20.	Ⓐ Ⓑ Ⓒ Ⓓ	26.	Ⓐ Ⓑ Ⓒ Ⓓ
3.	Ⓐ Ⓑ Ⓒ Ⓓ	9.	Ⓐ Ⓑ Ⓒ Ⓓ	15.	Ⓐ Ⓑ Ⓒ Ⓓ	21.	Ⓐ Ⓑ Ⓒ Ⓓ	27.	Ⓐ Ⓑ Ⓒ Ⓓ
4.	Ⓐ Ⓑ Ⓒ Ⓓ	10.	Ⓐ Ⓑ Ⓒ Ⓓ	16.	Ⓐ Ⓑ Ⓒ Ⓓ	22.	Ⓐ Ⓑ Ⓒ Ⓓ	28.	Ⓐ Ⓑ Ⓒ Ⓓ
5.	Ⓐ Ⓑ Ⓒ Ⓓ	11.	Ⓐ Ⓑ Ⓒ Ⓓ	17.	Ⓐ Ⓑ Ⓒ Ⓓ	23.	Ⓐ Ⓑ Ⓒ Ⓓ	29.	Ⓐ Ⓑ Ⓒ Ⓓ
6.	Ⓐ Ⓑ Ⓒ Ⓓ	12.	Ⓐ Ⓑ Ⓒ Ⓓ	18.	Ⓐ Ⓑ Ⓒ Ⓓ	24.	Ⓐ Ⓑ Ⓒ Ⓓ	30.	Ⓐ Ⓑ Ⓒ Ⓓ

LIGHT

LEARNING OBJECTIVES

- All sources of light
- A pinhole camera
- Lateral inversion
- The propagation of light
- Refraction and reflection of light
- The uses of spherical mirrors

MULTIPLE CHOICE QUESTIONS

1. A substance which transmits most of the light rays incident on it is called _______.
   (A) transparent
   (B) translucent
   (C) opaque
   (D) none of these

2. The distance between the sun and the earth is _______.
   (A) 1.2 light years
   (B) 2 billion kilometres
   (C) 150 million kilometers
   (D) 100 million kilometers

3. When the object is placed between C and F, the image is formed _______.
   (A) At C
   (B) At infinity
   (C) Behind the mirror
   (D) Beyond C

4. Light is _______.
   (A) mass less
   (B) a transverse wave
   (C) a electromagnetic radiation
   (D) all of these

5. The earth light can be seen from _______.
   (A) the sun
   (B) the moon
   (C) the earth
   (D) none of these

6. The speed of light is _______.
   (A) 330m/s
   (B) 300, 000, 000 m/s
   (C) 30,000 m/s
   (D) 300, 000, 000 km/s

7. The speed of light is _______.
   (A) the same in all media
   (B) greatest in vacuum
   (C) greater in air than in vacuum
   (D) does not change from medium to medium

8. Image formed by plane mirror is always _______.
   (A) real
   (B) inverted
   (C) virtual and enlarged
   (D) virtual and of same size

9. An image obtained on screen is _______.
   (A) real
   (B) inverted
   (C) both real and virtual
   (D) none of these

10. Which of the following letters will be seen without any change in a plane mirror?
    (A) P
    (B) L
    (C) T
    (D) S

11. A source of light is _______.
   (A) an object that can reflect light
   (B) an object that can refract light
   (C) an object that can absorb light
   (D) an object that can give light

12. As the distance of source increases _______.
   (A) intensity of light increases
   (B) intensity of light decreases
   (C) intensity of light remains the same
   (D) intensity of light may decrease or increase

13. Which of the following statement is true?
   (A) A plane mirror sometimes form an inverted image.
   (B) A concave mirror always forms a virtual, erect and diminished image.
   (C) A concave lens always forms a virtual, erect and diminished image.
   (D) None of these

14. A spherical mirror with its reflecting surface on the outside is a _______.
   (A) plane mirror
   (B) concave mirror
   (C) convex mirror
   (D) either concave or convex

15. Which of the following is non-luminous?
   (A) star   (B) sun
   (C) moon   (D) bulb

16. Which of the following is transparent?
   (A) stone   (B) wood
   (C) ground glass (D) plastic

17. Which of the following is opaque?
   (A) air   (B) vacuum
   (C) glass   (D) wood

18. Shadows are formed because _______.
   (A) light can bend around the opaque bodies.
   (B) light rays cannot pass through the opaque bodies.
   (C) opaque bodies allow the light to pass through them.
   (D) light shows the phenomenon of diffraction around large objects.

19. A magnifying glass is nothing but _______.
   (A) concave mirror
   (B) convex lens
   (C) concave lens
   (D) convex mirror

20. Which condition is true for virtual image?
   (A) it is always erect
   (B) it is formed behind the mirror
   (C) it can not be obtained on screen
   (D) all these conditions

21. A narrow stream of light is called a _______.
   (A) ray
   (B) beam
   (C) sunlight
   (D) none of these

22. A broad stream of light is called a _______.
   (A) ray
   (B) beam
   (C) twilight
   (D) sunlight

23. Radius of curvature for a plane mirror is _______.
   (A) positive
   (B) negative
   (C) infinity
   (D) none of these

24. The distance between the focus and the pole of the mirror is called _______.
   (A) focal length
   (B) principal axis
   (C) radius of curvature
   (D) diameter of curvature

25. In case of mirror match the columns A with columns B:

Column A	Column B
1. Centre of curvature	(A) Centre of the mirror
2. Focus	(B) Centre of the sphere of which the mirror is a part
3. Radius of curvature	(C) Point through which all the incident rays parallel to principle axis pass after reflection.
4. Principal axis	(D) Line joining the pole and focus
5. Pole	(E) Distance between pole and centre of curvature.

(A) 1 - B, 2 - C, 3 - A, 4 - E, 5 - D
(B) 1 - B, 2 - C, 3 - E, 4 - D, 5 - A
(C) 1 - C, 2 - B, 3 - A, 4 - D, 5 - E
(D) 1 - E, 2 - C, 3 - B, 4 - A, 5 - D

26. At a particular time of a day, the ratio of height of an object and the length of it's shadow is 'x'. Using this calculate the height of a tree if the length of the shadow of tree is L.

(A) $x + L$ (B) $x \times L$
(C) $L - x$ (D) $\dfrac{x}{L}$

27. Prism has _________.

(A) 3 surfaces   (B) 4 surfaces
(C) 5 surfaces   (D) 6 surfaces

28. A series of fast moving still pictures can create an illusion of movement because _________.

(A) eye is quicker than the brain
(B) the optical cortex can see through the rapidly moving images.
(C) the eye can focus on very rapidly changing pictures.
(D) eye can separate two images only when the interval of separation between them is one tenth of second.

29. In a periscope, the reflecting mirror will be _________.

(A) at an angle of 45°
(B) at an angle of 60°
(C) perpendicular to each other
(D) parallel to each other

30. Periscope is used to _________.

(A) view objects placed at a higher level from a position at lower level.
(B) magnify extremely small objects into bigger images.
(C) observe the distant images such as planets and stars.
(D) analyse the spectrum formed by the sunlight.

HOTS (ACHIEVERS SECTION)

Directions (31 – 35): Fill in the blanks with the appropriate option.

31. The objects that allow light to pass through them are called ___________.

(A) Transparent objects
(B) Luminous objects
(C) Translucent objects
(D) Non luminous objects

32. Light travels in straight path and this property of light is called _________.

(A) Luminosity
(B) Rectilinear propagation
(C) Lateral inversion
(D) Regular reflection

33. Any object kept in transparent circular container of water appears bigger than the actual size because water behaves as __________.
    (A) Concave lens   (B) Convex lens
    (C) Glass lab   (D) None of these

34. The colours in the rainbow are due to the property of light called __________.
    (A) Rectilinear propagation
    (B) Reflection
    (C) Dispersion
    (D) Refraction

35. Which of the following is not a translucent object?
    (A) Greased paper   (B) Paraffin wax
    (C) Frosted glass   (D) Torch light

36. At a particular time, the constant of ratio of length of a light pole and the length of its shadow is found to be 2.5 m. Now, the length of the shadow of a flag pole is 25 m, calculate the length of the pole.
    (A) 62.5 m   (B) 22.5 m
    (C) 2.25 m   (D) 13.5 m

37. We can create enlarged, virtual images with __________.
    (A) Concave lens
    (B) Concave mirrors
    (C) Plane mirrors
    (D) Convex mirrors

38. In which circuit will the bulb glow the brightest?
    (A) A simple circuit with one bulb and one cell
    (B) A simple circuit with two bulbs and two cells
    (C) A simple circuit with two bulbs and one cell
    (D) A simple circuit with one bulb and two cells

39. Boojho and Paheli were given one mirror each by their teacher. Boojho found his image to be erect and of the same size, whereas Paheli found her image erect and smaller in size. This means that the mirrors of Boojho and Paheli respectively are:
    (A) plane mirror and concave mirror
    (B) concave mirror and convex mirror
    (C) plane mirror and convex mirror
    (D) convex mirror and plane mirror

40. Which of the following always diverge light rays?
    (A) Convex mirror and plane mirror
    (B) Concave lens and convex mirror
    (C) Concave mirror and convex lens
    (D) Concave lens and convex mirror

———Darken Your Choice with HB Pencil———

1.	Ⓐ Ⓑ Ⓒ Ⓓ	9.	Ⓐ Ⓑ Ⓒ Ⓓ	17.	Ⓐ Ⓑ Ⓒ Ⓓ	25	Ⓐ Ⓑ Ⓒ Ⓓ	33.	Ⓐ Ⓑ Ⓒ Ⓓ
2.	Ⓐ Ⓑ Ⓒ Ⓓ	10.	Ⓐ Ⓑ Ⓒ Ⓓ	18.	Ⓐ Ⓑ Ⓒ Ⓓ	26.	Ⓐ Ⓑ Ⓒ Ⓓ	34.	Ⓐ Ⓑ Ⓒ Ⓓ
3.	Ⓐ Ⓑ Ⓒ Ⓓ	11.	Ⓐ Ⓑ Ⓒ Ⓓ	19.	Ⓐ Ⓑ Ⓒ Ⓓ	27.	Ⓐ Ⓑ Ⓒ Ⓓ	35.	Ⓐ Ⓑ Ⓒ Ⓓ
4.	Ⓐ Ⓑ Ⓒ Ⓓ	12.	Ⓐ Ⓑ Ⓒ Ⓓ	20.	Ⓐ Ⓑ Ⓒ Ⓓ	28.	Ⓐ Ⓑ Ⓒ Ⓓ	36.	Ⓐ Ⓑ Ⓒ Ⓓ
5.	Ⓐ Ⓑ Ⓒ Ⓓ	13.	Ⓐ Ⓑ Ⓒ Ⓓ	21.	Ⓐ Ⓑ Ⓒ Ⓓ	29.	Ⓐ Ⓑ Ⓒ Ⓓ	37.	Ⓐ Ⓑ Ⓒ Ⓓ
6.	Ⓐ Ⓑ Ⓒ Ⓓ	14.	Ⓐ Ⓑ Ⓒ Ⓓ	22.	Ⓐ Ⓑ Ⓒ Ⓓ	30	Ⓐ Ⓑ Ⓒ Ⓓ	38.	Ⓐ Ⓑ Ⓒ Ⓓ
7.	Ⓐ Ⓑ Ⓒ Ⓓ	15.	Ⓐ Ⓑ Ⓒ Ⓓ	23.	Ⓐ Ⓑ Ⓒ Ⓓ	31.	Ⓐ Ⓑ Ⓒ Ⓓ	39.	Ⓐ Ⓑ Ⓒ Ⓓ
8.	Ⓐ Ⓑ Ⓒ Ⓓ	16.	Ⓐ Ⓑ Ⓒ Ⓓ	24.	Ⓐ Ⓑ Ⓒ Ⓓ	32.	Ⓐ Ⓑ Ⓒ Ⓓ	40.	Ⓐ Ⓑ Ⓒ Ⓓ

LOGICAL REASONING 

LEARNING OBJECTIVES

- Different types of patterns
- Concept of number series
- Concept of alphabetical series
- Concept of classification and its different types
- Concept of Coding and Decoding
- Alphabet Test concepts
- Concept of Letter word problems
- Different types of blood relation
- Different directions and their concept
- Number test
- Ranking test
- Concept of Odd one out
- Different rules for Dice based questions
- Mirror image of letters
- Mirror image of numbers
- Water image of letters
- Water image of numbers
- Concept of embedded figures
- Different types of Venn diagram

MULTIPLE CHOICE QUESTIONS

Directions (1–3): Choose the appropriate number which follows the given pattern.

1.

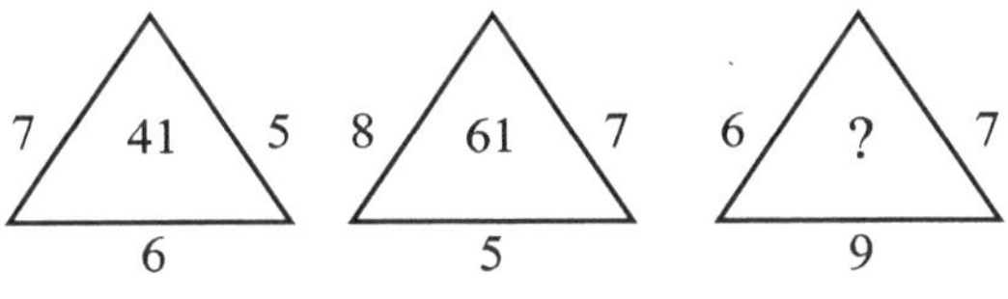

(A) 61   (B) 71

(C) 51   (D) 59

2.

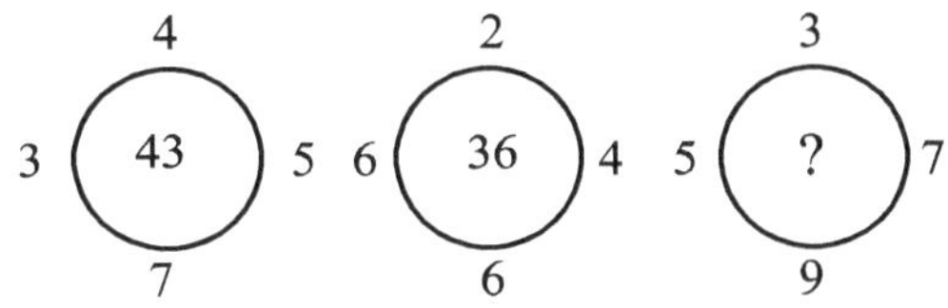

(A) 62   (B) 52

(C) 72   (D) 82

3.

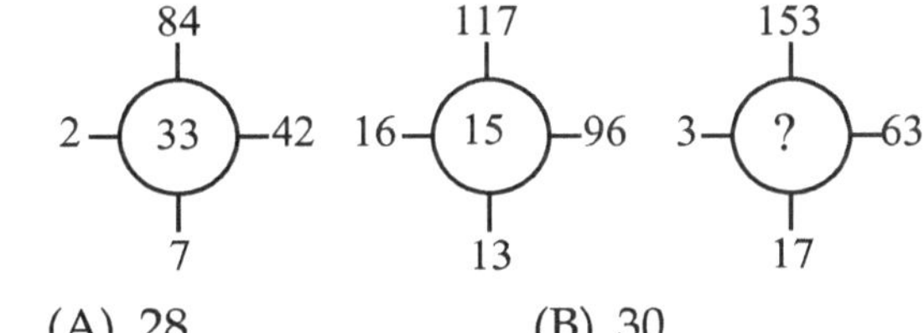

(A) 28   (B) 30

(C) 31   (D) 32

Directions (4–6): In each of the following questions, a number series is given with one missing term. Choose correct alternative that will continue the same pattern and fill in the blank spaces.

4. 1000, 200, 40, ——.

(A) 8   (B) 10

(C) 15   (D) 20

5. 5.2, 4.8, 4.4, 4, ______.
   (A) 3   (B) 3.3
   (C) 3.5   (D) 3.6

6. 2, 6, 18, 54, ______.
   (A) 108   (B) 148
   (C) 162   (D) 216

Directions (7–9): In each of the following letter series, some of the letters are missing, which are given in such order as one of the alternatives below it. Choose the correct alternative.

7. _ op _ mo _ n _ _ pnmop _.
   (A) mnpmon   (B) mpnmop
   (C) mnompn   (D) mnpomn

8. _bcc _ ac _ aabb _ ab _ cc
   (A) aabca   (B) abaca
   (C) bacab   (D) bcaca

9. m _ nm _ n _ an _ a _ ma _
   (A) aamnan   (B) ammanm
   (C) aammnn   (D) amammn

Directions (10–12): Find the odd one out and choose the correct option.

10. 3, 5, 7, 12, 17, 19
    (A) 19   (B) 17
    (C) 5   (D) 12

11. 41, 43, 47, 53, 61, 71, 73, 81
    (A) 61   (B) 71
    (C) 73   (D) 81

12. 835, 734, 642, 751, 853, 981, 532
    (A) 751   (B) 853
    (C) 981   (D) 532

13. In a certain language, SIGHT is written as FVTUC, how is REVEAL written in the same language?
    (A) ERIRNY   (B) DQHQMX
    (C) FSJSOZ   (D) YNRIRE

14. If in a certain language, MADRAS is coded as NBESBT, how is BOMBAY coded in that language?
    (A) CPNCBZ   (B) CPNCBX
    (C) CPOCBZ   (D) CQOCBZ

15. In a certain code, ROAD is written URDG, how is SWAN written in that code?
    (A) VZCP   (B) UXDQ
    (C) VZDQ   (D) VXDQ

Directions (16–18): Arrange the given words in alphabetical order and choose the one that comes first.

16. (A) waving   (B) watching
    (C) waiting   (D) wanting

17. (A) Lapse   (B) Leave
    (C) Leisure   (D) Laurel

18. (A) Protein   (B) Proverb
    (C) Property   (D) Project

19. Pointing to a man on the stage, Ritu said, "He is the brother of the daughter of the wife of my husband." How is the man on the stage related to Ritu?
    (A) Husband   (B) Cousin
    (C) Nephew   (D) Son

20. A party consists of grandmother, father, mother, four sons and their wives and one son and two daughters to each of the sons. How many females are there in all?
    (A) 14   (B) 19
    (C) 12   (D) 25

21. Lata and Mona are Ravi's wives. Shalu is Mona's Step-daughter. How is Lata related to Shalu?
    (A) Sister
    (B) Mother-in-Law
    (C) Mother
    (D) Step-mother

22. From his house, Lokesh went 15 km to the North. Then he turned west and covered 10 km. Then he turned south and covered 5 km. Finally turning to the east, he covered 10 km. In which direction is he from his house?
    (A) East   (B) West
    (C) North   (D) South

23. Sachin walks 20 km towards North. He turns left and walks 40 km. He again turns left and walks 20 km. Finally he moves 20 km after turning to the left. How far is he from his starting position?

   (A) 20 km   (B) 30 km
   (C) 50 km   (D) 60 km

24. Sundar runs 20 m towards East and turns to right and runs 10 m. Then he turns to the right and runs 9 m. Again he turns to right and runs 5 m. After this he turns to left and runs 12 m and finally he turns to right and moves 6 m. Now to which direction is Sundar facing?

   (A) East   (B) West
   (C) North   (D) South

Directions (25–27): Study the given number series and answer the questions based on it.

5 7 8 9 7 6 5 3 4 2 6 8 9 7 5 2 4 6 2 9 7 6 4 7 8 9 7 6

25. How many 7s are preceded by 9 and followed by 6?

   (A) 1   (B) 2
   (C) 3   (D) 4

26. Which digits have equal frequency?

   (A) 2, 5, 8   (B) 2, 5, 6
   (C) 4, 5, 9   (D) 3, 4, 9

27. Which digit has highest frequency?

   (A) 5   (B) 6
   (C) 7   (D) 9

Directions (28–30): In each problem, out of the five figures marked (1), (2), (3), (4) and (5), four are similar in a certain manner. However, one figure is not like the other four. Choose the figure which is different from the rest.

28. 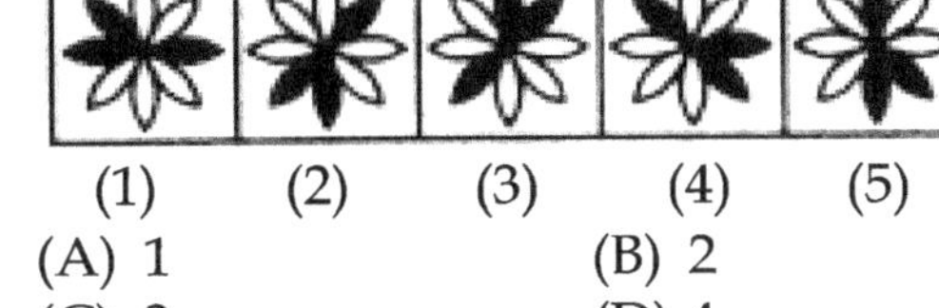

    (1)   (2)   (3)   (4)   (5)
   (A) 1   (B) 2
   (C) 3   (D) 4
   (e) 5

29. 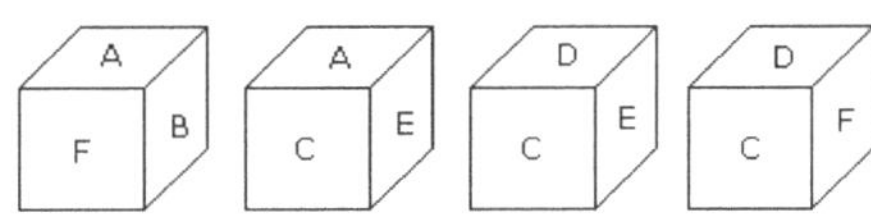

    (1)   (2)   (3)   (4)   (5)
   (A) 1   (B) 2
   (C) 3   (D) 4
   (e) 5

30. 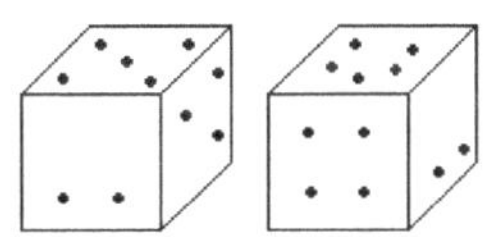

    (1)   (2)   (3)   (4)   (5)
   (A) 1   (B) 2
   (C) 3   (D) 4
   (e) 5

31. The positions of a cube are shown below, Which letter will be on the face opposite to face with 'A'?

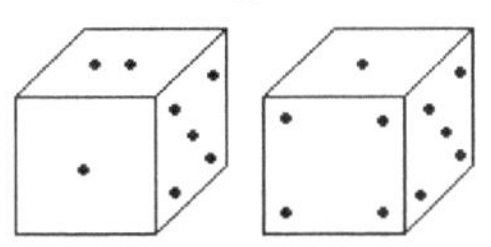

   (A) D   (B) B
   (C) C   (D) F

32. Two positions of a dice are shown below. When 3 points are at the bottom, how many points will be at the top?

   (A) 2   (B) 5
   (C) 4   (D) 6

33. Observe the dots on the dice (one to six dots) in the following figures. How many dots are contained on the face opposite to the face containing four dots?

   (A) 2   (B) 3
   (C) 5   (D) 6

Directions (34–36): In each of the following questions you are given a combination of alphabets and/or numbers followed by four alternatives (1), (2), (3) and (4).

34. Choose the alternative which closely resembles the mirror-image of the given combination.

    UTZFY6KH

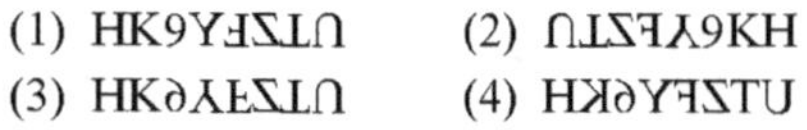

    (1) HK9YᖷZTU　　(2) ∩⊥ZꟻY9KH

    (3) HKᓯYꟻZT∩　　(4) HꓘᓯYꟻƧTU

    (A) 1　　　　　　(B) 2
    (C) 3　　　　　　(D) 4

35. Choose the alternative which closely resembles the mirror-image of the given combination.

    AN54WMG3

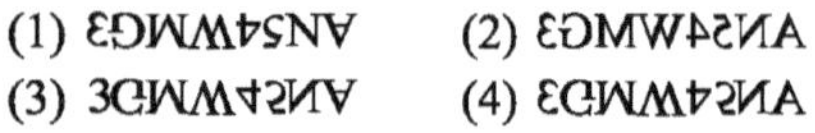

    (1) ƐƆWM�480NA　　(2) ƐƆMWᘉᔕᴙA

    (3) 3ƆWMᘈᔕ∀A　　(4) ƐƆWMᘈᔕᴎA

    (A) 1　　　　　　(B) 2
    (C) 3　　　　　　(D) 4

36. Choose the alternative which closely resembles the mirror-image of the given combination.

    SUPERVISOR

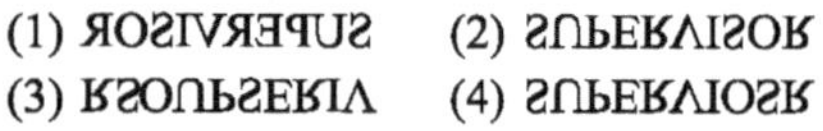

    (1) ᴙOᔕIVᴙƎꟼUƧ　　(2) ƧUᴘᴇᴙᴧIƧOᴙ

    (3) ᴙƧOᴘᴇᴙᴧIᴧ　　(4) ƧUᴘᴇᴙᴧIOᔕᴙ

    (A) 1　　　　　　(B) 2
    (C) 3　　　　　　(D) 4

Directions (37–39): In each of the following questions, choose the water image of the Fig. (X) from amongst the four alternatives (1), (2), (3) and (4) given along with it.

37. Choose the alternative which closely resembles the water-image of the given figure (X).

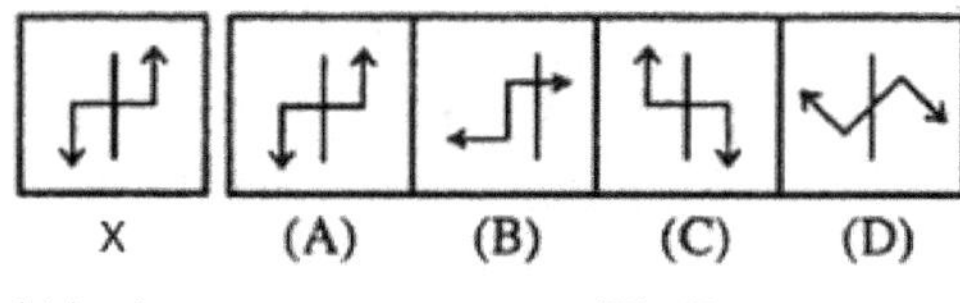

(A) A　　　　　　(B) B
(C) C　　　　　　(D) D

38. Choose the alternative which closely resembles the water-image of the given figure (X).

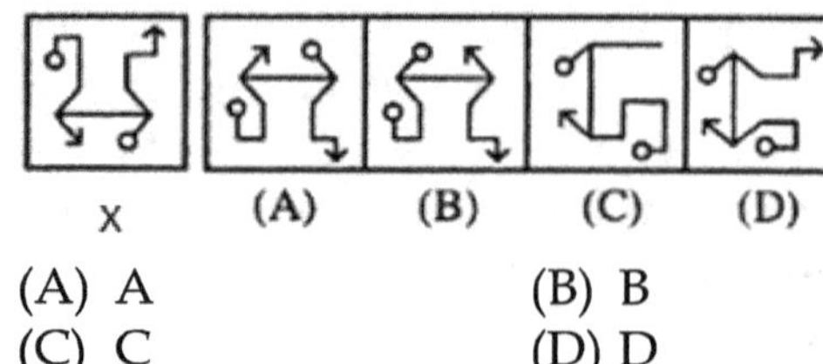

(A) A　　　　　　(B) B
(C) C　　　　　　(D) D

39. Choose the alternative which closely resembles the water-image of the given figure (X).

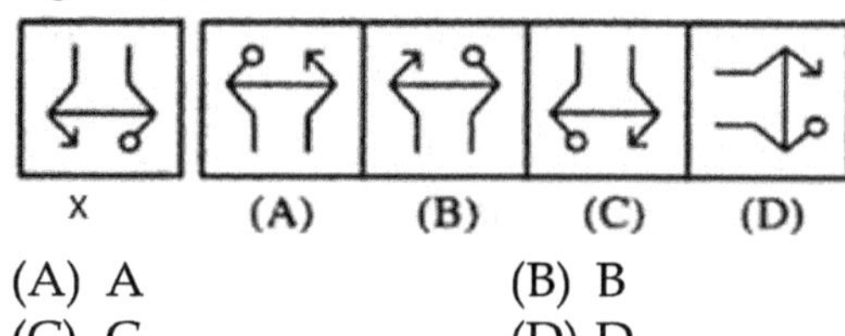

(A) A　　　　　　(B) B
(C) C　　　　　　(D) D

Directions (40–42): In each of the following questions, you are given a figure (X) followed by four alternative figures (A), (B), (C) and (D) such that figure (X) is embedded in one of them. Find out the alternative figure which contains fig. (X) as its part.

40. Find out the alternative figure which contains figure (X) as its part.

Figure　Answer Figures

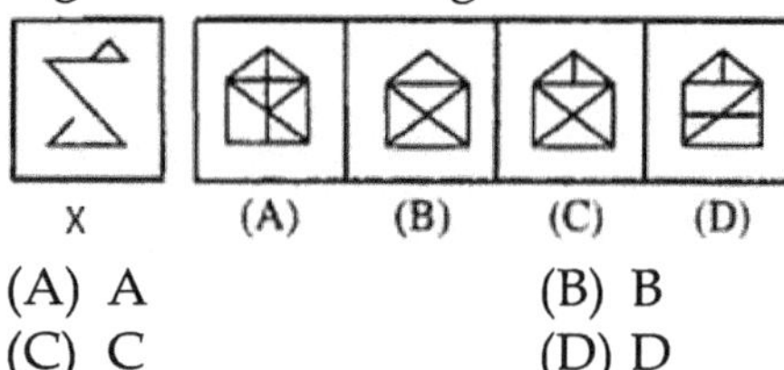

(A) A　　　　　　(B) B
(C) C　　　　　　(D) D

41. Find out the alternative figure which contains figure (X) as its part.

Figure　Answer Figures

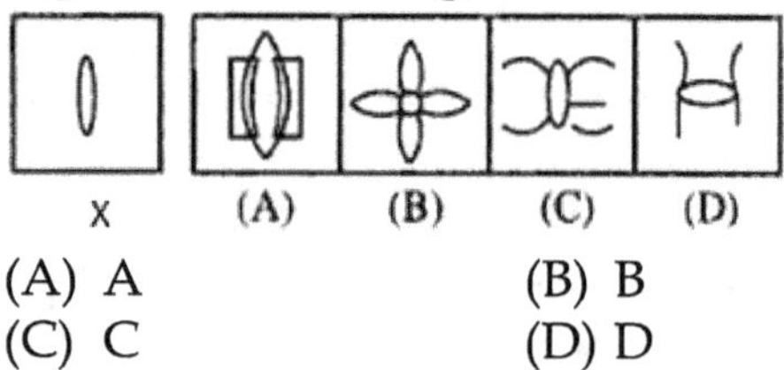

(A) A　　　　　　(B) B
(C) C　　　　　　(D) D

42. Find out the alternative figure which contains figure (X) as its part.

Figure　Answer Figures

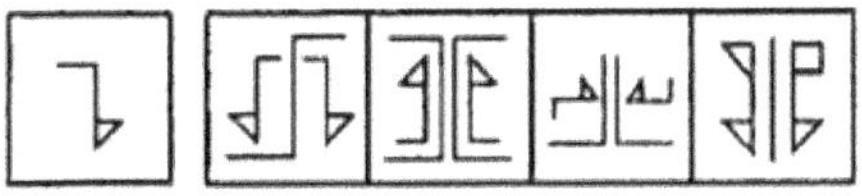

X (A) (B) (C) (D)

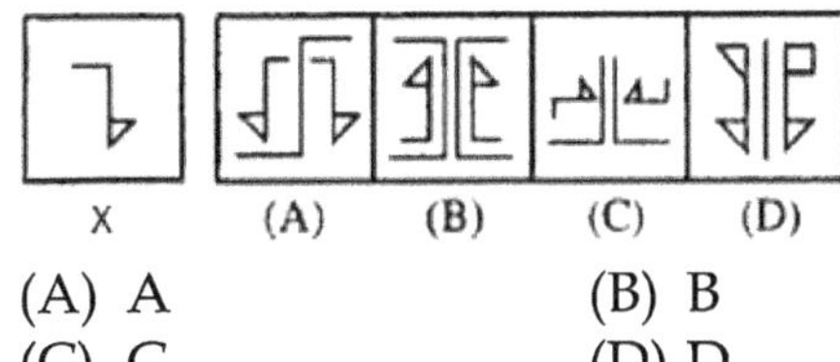

(A) A (B) B
(C) C (D) D

Directions (43–45): Each of these questions contains three elements. These elements may or may not have some inter linkage. Each group of elements may fit into one of these diagrams at (A), (B), (C), (D). You have to choose the group of elements which correctly fits into the diagrams.

43. Which of the following diagrams indicates the best relation among Author, Lawyer and Singer?

(A)  (B) 

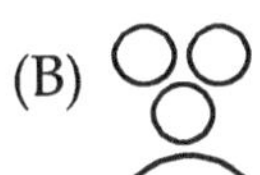

(C)  (D) 

44. Which of the following diagrams indicates the best relation among Factory, Product and Machinery?

(A)  (B) 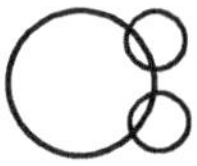

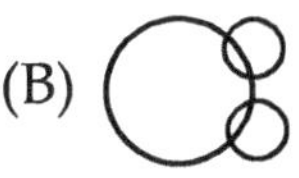

(C)  (D) 

45. Which of the following diagrams indicates the best relation among Women, Mothers and Engineers?

(A) 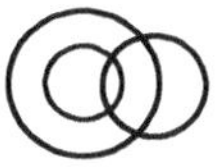 (B) 

(C)  (D) 

Darken Your Choice with HB Pencil

1.	Ⓐ	Ⓑ	Ⓒ	Ⓓ	10.	Ⓐ	Ⓑ	Ⓒ	Ⓓ	19.	Ⓐ	Ⓑ	Ⓒ	Ⓓ	28	Ⓐ	Ⓑ	Ⓒ	Ⓓ	37	Ⓐ	Ⓑ	Ⓒ	Ⓓ
2.	Ⓐ	Ⓑ	Ⓒ	Ⓓ	11.	Ⓐ	Ⓑ	Ⓒ	Ⓓ	20.	Ⓐ	Ⓑ	Ⓒ	Ⓓ	29.	Ⓐ	Ⓑ	Ⓒ	Ⓓ	38.	Ⓐ	Ⓑ	Ⓒ	Ⓓ
3.	Ⓐ	Ⓑ	Ⓒ	Ⓓ	12.	Ⓐ	Ⓑ	Ⓒ	Ⓓ	21.	Ⓐ	Ⓑ	Ⓒ	Ⓓ	30.	Ⓐ	Ⓑ	Ⓒ	Ⓓ	39.	Ⓐ	Ⓑ	Ⓒ	Ⓓ
4.	Ⓐ	Ⓑ	Ⓒ	Ⓓ	13.	Ⓐ	Ⓑ	Ⓒ	Ⓓ	22.	Ⓐ	Ⓑ	Ⓒ	Ⓓ	31.	Ⓐ	Ⓑ	Ⓒ	Ⓓ	40.	Ⓐ	Ⓑ	Ⓒ	Ⓓ
5.	Ⓐ	Ⓑ	Ⓒ	Ⓓ	14.	Ⓐ	Ⓑ	Ⓒ	Ⓓ	23.	Ⓐ	Ⓑ	Ⓒ	Ⓓ	32.	Ⓐ	Ⓑ	Ⓒ	Ⓓ	41.	Ⓐ	Ⓑ	Ⓒ	Ⓓ
6.	Ⓐ	Ⓑ	Ⓒ	Ⓓ	15.	Ⓐ	Ⓑ	Ⓒ	Ⓓ	24.	Ⓐ	Ⓑ	Ⓒ	Ⓓ	33	Ⓐ	Ⓑ	Ⓒ	Ⓓ	42.	Ⓐ	Ⓑ	Ⓒ	Ⓓ
7.	Ⓐ	Ⓑ	Ⓒ	Ⓓ	16.	Ⓐ	Ⓑ	Ⓒ	Ⓓ	25.	Ⓐ	Ⓑ	Ⓒ	Ⓓ	34.	Ⓐ	Ⓑ	Ⓒ	Ⓓ	43.	Ⓐ	Ⓑ	Ⓒ	Ⓓ
8.	Ⓐ	Ⓑ	Ⓒ	Ⓓ	17.	Ⓐ	Ⓑ	Ⓒ	Ⓓ	26.	Ⓐ	Ⓑ	Ⓒ	Ⓓ	35.	Ⓐ	Ⓑ	Ⓒ	Ⓓ	44.	Ⓐ	Ⓑ	Ⓒ	Ⓓ
9.	Ⓐ	Ⓑ	Ⓒ	Ⓓ	18.	Ⓐ	Ⓑ	Ⓒ	Ⓓ	27.	Ⓐ	Ⓑ	Ⓒ	Ⓓ	36.	Ⓐ	Ⓑ	Ⓒ	Ⓓ	45.	Ⓐ	Ⓑ	Ⓒ	Ⓓ

MODEL TEST PAPER

1. If O = 16, FOR = 42, then what is FRONT equal to
   (A) 78   (B) 65
   (C) 73   (D) 61

2. Choose the odd one out.
   (A) VRT   (B) RMP
   (C) YUM   (D) FBD

3. Choose the alternative which closely resembles the water-image of the given combination.

   MNOP

   A. ШИОР   B. PONM
   C. ШИОЬ   D. MNOP

   (A) A   (B) B
   (C) C   (D) D

4. Prakash is the son of Pramod. Neha is the daughter of Abhishek. Ruchi is the mother of Neha. Awadhesh is the brother of Neha. How is Awadhesh related to Ruchi?
   (A) Brother
   (B) Father
   (C) Son
   (D) Can not be determined

Direction (5 to 6): In the questions given below, a number series is given with one missing term Choose the correct alternative that will continue the same pattern and fill in the blank spaces.

5. 625, 5, 125, 25, 25, _______, 5.
   (A) 5   (B) 25
   (C) 125   (D) 625

6. 240, _______, 120, 40, 10, 2
   (A) 180   (B) 240
   (C) 420   (D) 480

7. X started to walk straight towards south. After waking 5 m he turned to the left and walked 3 m. After this he turned to the right and walked 5 m. Now to which direction X is facing?
   (A) North-East   (B) South
   (C) North   (D) South-West

8. A boy rides his bicycle northward, then turned left and rode 1 km and again turned left and rode 2 km. He found himself 1 km west of his starting point. How far did he ride northward initially?
   (A) 1 km   (B) 2 km
   (C) 3 km   (D) 5 km

9. Sukesh and Rajesh are ranked 6th and 13th respectively from the top in a class of 71 students. What will be their respective position from the bottom in the class?
   (A) 65 and 59   (B) 66 and 58
   (C) 66 and 59   (D) 67 and 59

10. Sujata is 8 ranks ahead of Sunita who ranks 23rd in a class of 50 students. What is Sujata's rank from the last?
    (A) 33rd   (B) 34th
    (C) 35th   (D) 36th

11. The light from the sun takes 500s to reach the earth. Assuming that the speed of light is 3,00,000 km/s, calculate the distance between the sun and the earth.
    (A) 100 million km
    (B) 150 million km
    (C) 200 million km
    (D) 300 million km

12. A spectrum is obtained by sending a beam of white light through a prism. A second prism exactly similar to the first one is placed in an inverted position with the sides parallel to first. Now ______.
    (A) a new spectrum will be formed on the screen with double the number of colours present in the previous spectrum.
    (B) new spectrum will be obtained on the screen with only half the number of colours present in the previous spectrum.
    (C) a spectrum with same number of colours present in the previous spectrum will be formed but their wave lengths will be increased twice.
    (D) previous spectrum will disappear and we will obtain a white light formed by the fusion of the colours.

13. The time period of a pendulum depends upon ______.
    (A) the mass of the bob
    (B) the length of the pendulum
    (C) the material of the bob
    (D) the size of the bob

14. A car travelled a distance of 200 km between Delhi and Agra in 2.5 hours. Calculate the average speed of the car during the journey.
    (A) 20 km/hr   (B) 40 km/hr
    (C) 80 km/hr   (D) 160 km/hr

15. According to the law of conservation of energy ______.
    (A) energy exists in many forms but it cannot be transformed.
    (B) energy exists in only one form.
    (C) energy can be created but not destroyed, and it can be transformed from one form to another.
    (D) energy can neither be produced nor be destroyed and it can be transformed from one form to another form.

16. Chemical reactions produce heat energy if ______.
    (A) energy absorbed by reactants is less than the energy released by products.
    (B) energy absorbed by reactants is more than the energy released by products.
    (C) energy absorbed by reactants is equal to the energy released by products.
    (D) all of these

17. The wire used in a fuse has ______.
    (A) low melting point
    (B) high melting point
    (C) average melting point
    (D) all of these

18. What is overloading?
    (A) touching of live wire with the earth wire.
    (B) touching of live wire with the neutral wire
    (C) touching of neutral wire with the earth wire
    (D) drawing extremely large amount of current from the single household circuit

19. Which one of the following is obtained from tree for the making of litmus?
    (A) banyan   (B) lichen
    (C) peepal   (D) all the these

20. A rose is used as an indicator in the chemical laboratory. Name it.
    (A) red rose   (B) white rose
    (C) blue rose   (D) China rose

21. Pure crystals of salt are obtained by ______.
    (A) melting   (B) boiling
    (C) evaporation   (D) diffusion

22. The density of water is greatest at ______.
    (A) 0°C   (B) 4°C
    (C) 37°C   (D) 100°C

23. Our body temperature is maintained at ______.
    (A) 11°C   (B) 20°C
    (C) 37°C   (D) 41°C

24. The density of water is _______.
(A) 0.5g/cm^3 (B) 0.1 g/cm^3
(C) 1 g/cm^3 (D) 10 g/cm^3

25. Which property of water is used while washing clothes?
(A) odour (B) solubility
(C) colour (D) none of these

26. When we destroy a forest, we destroy _______.
(A) an ecosystem
(B) the plant life
(C) food and shelter of wild animals
(D) population of wild life

27. Soil erosion can occur due to _______.
(A) rains or floods
(B) deforestation
(C) high velocity winds
(D) all the above

28. Plants in cold regions shed leaves because of _______.
(A) cold weather (B) longer nights
(C) water scarcity (D) shorter days

29. A leaf insect looks like leaves and polar bear living in snowy regions has white fur on its skin. Although these animals are very different from each other, what is the one way in which they are similar?
(A) They use their bodies to prepare food.
(B) They use their bodies to attack enemies.
(C) They use their bodies to confuse enemies.
(D) They migrate to long distance to protect themselves from enemies.

30. Excretory waste of fish is _______.
(A) ammonia (B) urea
(C) uric acid (D) salts

31. Which of the following bacteria causes sorter's disease in sorter's?
(A) cauliform (B) clostridium
(C) rhizobium (D) anthrax

32. A fungus growing on stale bread is _______.

(A) symbiont (B) saprophyte
(C) insectivorus (D) parasite

33. A number of steps in holozoic nutrition in animals are _______.
(A) 2 (B) 3
(C) 4 (D) 5

34. After digestion process, the digested food is _______.
(A) removed (B) assimilated
(C) absorbed (D) none of these

35. Blood vessels and nerves of a tooth are present in _______.
(A) dentine
(B) pulp cavity
(C) enamel
(D) crown of a tooth

36. The longest part of the alimentary canal is _______.
(A) small intestine (B) large intestine
(C) oesophagus (D) stomach

37. Lenticels are found in _______.
(A) the root where secondary growth has occured.
(B) the stem in which secondary growth has taken place.
(C) the roots as well as the stem where secondary growth has occurred
(D) none of the above

38. Why do whales and dolphins often come upto the water surface?
(A) to get food
(B) to swim
(C) to breathe
(D) to get sufficient sunlight

39. When haemoglobin combines with oxygen, the compound formed is _______.
(A) haemoglobide
(B) haemoglobic oxide
(C) haemoglobin oxide
(D) oxyhaemoglobin

40. Red blood cells are ____ white blood cells in size.
(A) equal to (B) larger than
(C) smaller than (D) none of these

41. The right side of the heart ———.
   (A) receives blood from the lungs
   (B) receives blood from the rest of the body
   (C) pumps blood to the rest of the body
   (D) none of these

42. Fast moving air produces ———.
   (A) cyclone   (B) disaster
   (C) storm   (D) rain

43. The length of Indian coastline is approximately ____ km.
   (A) 6,715   (B) 8,571
   (C) 6,915   (D) 7,751

44. Potato is a ———.
   (A) root   (B) stem
   (C) tuber   (D) leaf

45. ______ is a ripened ovary.
   (A) Seed   (B) Embryo
   (C) Fruit   (D) All of these

46. Anaerobic bacteria digest animal waste and produce biogas (change - A). The biogas then burns as fuel (change - B), the following statements pertain to these changes. Choose the correct one.
   (A) Process – A is a chemical change
   (B) Process – B is a physical change
   (C) Both processes A and B are chemical changes
   (D) None of these processes is a chemical change

Direction (47 – 49): Fill in the blanks with appropriate options.

47. ________ is necessary for tissue oxidation.
   (A) Phosphorous   (B) Iodine
   (C) Sodium   (D) Iron

48. ______ filter the blood and collect the wastes in kidneys.
   (A) Veins
   (B) Nephron
   (C) Ureters
   (D) Urinary bladders

49. Tropical rain forests are found in _____ Ghats and ____ in India.
   (A) Eastern, Rajasthan
   (B) Eastern, Himachal Pradesh
   (C) Western, Assam
   (D) All of these

50. Breathing cannot be considered as a whole process of respiration because ______.
   (A) Oxidation of food does not come under it.
   (B) Only some parts of respiratory system are involved in breathing.
   (C) Breathing does not take part in transporting waste material out of body.
   (D) All of these

————Darken Your Choice with HB Pencil————

1.	Ⓐ Ⓑ Ⓒ Ⓓ	11.	Ⓐ Ⓑ Ⓒ Ⓓ	21.	Ⓐ Ⓑ Ⓒ Ⓓ	31	Ⓐ Ⓑ Ⓒ Ⓓ	41.	Ⓐ Ⓑ Ⓒ Ⓓ
2.	Ⓐ Ⓑ Ⓒ Ⓓ	12.	Ⓐ Ⓑ Ⓒ Ⓓ	22.	Ⓐ Ⓑ Ⓒ Ⓓ	32.	Ⓐ Ⓑ Ⓒ Ⓓ	42.	Ⓐ Ⓑ Ⓒ Ⓓ
3.	Ⓐ Ⓑ Ⓒ Ⓓ	13.	Ⓐ Ⓑ Ⓒ Ⓓ	23.	Ⓐ Ⓑ Ⓒ Ⓓ	33.	Ⓐ Ⓑ Ⓒ Ⓓ	43.	Ⓐ Ⓑ Ⓒ Ⓓ
4.	Ⓐ Ⓑ Ⓒ Ⓓ	14.	Ⓐ Ⓑ Ⓒ Ⓓ	24.	Ⓐ Ⓑ Ⓒ Ⓓ	34.	Ⓐ Ⓑ Ⓒ Ⓓ	44.	Ⓐ Ⓑ Ⓒ Ⓓ
5.	Ⓐ Ⓑ Ⓒ Ⓓ	15.	Ⓐ Ⓑ Ⓒ Ⓓ	25.	Ⓐ Ⓑ Ⓒ Ⓓ	35.	Ⓐ Ⓑ Ⓒ Ⓓ	45.	Ⓐ Ⓑ Ⓒ Ⓓ
6.	Ⓐ Ⓑ Ⓒ Ⓓ	16.	Ⓐ Ⓑ Ⓒ Ⓓ	26.	Ⓐ Ⓑ Ⓒ Ⓓ	36.	Ⓐ Ⓑ Ⓒ Ⓓ	46.	Ⓐ Ⓑ Ⓒ Ⓓ
7.	Ⓐ Ⓑ Ⓒ Ⓓ	17.	Ⓐ Ⓑ Ⓒ Ⓓ	27.	Ⓐ Ⓑ Ⓒ Ⓓ	37.	Ⓐ Ⓑ Ⓒ Ⓓ	47.	Ⓐ Ⓑ Ⓒ Ⓓ
8.	Ⓐ Ⓑ Ⓒ Ⓓ	18.	Ⓐ Ⓑ Ⓒ Ⓓ	28.	Ⓐ Ⓑ Ⓒ Ⓓ	38.	Ⓐ Ⓑ Ⓒ Ⓓ	48.	Ⓐ Ⓑ Ⓒ Ⓓ
9.	Ⓐ Ⓑ Ⓒ Ⓓ	19.	Ⓐ Ⓑ Ⓒ Ⓓ	29.	Ⓐ Ⓑ Ⓒ Ⓓ	39.	Ⓐ Ⓑ Ⓒ Ⓓ	49.	Ⓐ Ⓑ Ⓒ Ⓓ
10.	Ⓐ Ⓑ Ⓒ Ⓓ	20.	Ⓐ Ⓑ Ⓒ Ⓓ	30.	Ⓐ Ⓑ Ⓒ Ⓓ	40.	Ⓐ Ⓑ Ⓒ Ⓓ	50.	Ⓐ Ⓑ Ⓒ Ⓓ

HINTS AND SOLUTIONS

1. NUTRITION IN PLANTS & ANIMALS

Answer Key

1. (D)	2. (C)	3. (C)	4. (A)	5. (B)	6. (C)	7. (B)	8. (C)	9. (B)	10. (C)
11. (C)	12. (D)	13. (A)	14. (A)	15. (B)	16. (D)	17. (B)	18. (C)	19. (A)	20. (C)
21. (B)	22. (B)	23. (A)	24. (A)	25. (B)					

8. (C)
Cuscuta is a parasitic plant. It lacks chlorophyll, hence it appears as yellow tubular structure and obtains its food from its host mulberry.

9. (B)
Croton plants have chlorophyll but other red pigments are more in number than the chlorophyll so they are not in green colour. But they can perform photosynthesis.

15. (B)

The digestion taking place in small intestine is extracellular digestion.

20. (C)
Sunlight is essential for photosynthesis as the plant is kept in dark room for a week. There is a lack of sunlight, hence photosynthesis has not taken place.

21. (B)
Pulp is the soft material in the tooth. It is richly supplied with blood vessels and nerves.

HOTS (ACHIEVERS SECTION)

26. (A)	27. (B)	28. (A)	29. (B)	30. (B)

2. FIBRE TO FABRIC

Answer Key

1. (A)	2. (B)	3. (A)	4. (D)	5. (A)	6. (B)	7. (C)	8. (B)	9. (C)	10. (B)
11. (A)	12. (D)	13. (A)	14. (B)	15. (B)	16. (A)	17. (B)	18. (C)	19. (A)	20. (D)
21. (B)	22. (A)	23. (B)	24. (B)	25. (D)					

3. (A)
Silk moths feed only on mulberry leaves, hence these silk moths are also called as mulberry silk moths.

7. (C)
Hair trap a lot of air and it keeps animal warm.

15. (B)

Scouring is done after shearing the skin with fur. In scouring, the skin with fur is washed thoroughly in tanks to remove grease, dust and dirt.

18. (C)
Head is swinged from side to side during the formation of cocoon around the caterpillar.

20. (D)
The process of taking out threads from the cocoon for use as silk is called as reeling.

22. (A)
Lohi bread yield good quality wool. It is found in the states of Rajasthan and Punjab.

HOTS (ACHIEVERS SECTION)

26. (C)	27. (C)	28. (A)	29. (D)	30. (B)

30. (B)
Scouring is done after shearing the skin with fur. In scouring, the skin is washed thoroughly in tanks to remove grease, dust and dirt from the fur.

3. HEAT AND TEMPERATURE

Answer Key

1. (C)	2. (C)	3. (D)	4. (D)	5. (B)	6. (B)	7. (B)	8. (B)	9. (A)	10. (B)
11. (C)	12. (D)	13. (D)	14. (B)	15. (A)	16. (D)	17. (B)	18. (C)	19. (D)	20. (C)
21. (C)	22. (C)	23. (A)	24. (B)	25. (D)					

5. (B)
Alcohol has a freezing point much lower than other given substances here.

6. (B)
1 cal = 4.18 joules.

8. (B)
Heat always flows from a hotter region to a colder region. Since iron is a good conductor of heat, more heat will flow from our body to it and we will feel cold. As paper is a bad conductor, less heat will flow from our body.

9. (A)
The lower fixed point in the Celsius scale is 0°C, which is the melting point of ice.

10. (B)
The upper fixed point in the Celsius scale is 100°C, which is the boiling point of water.

11. (C)
The chemicals present in the candle burn with oxygen to give out heat.

13. (D)
Metals are better conductors of heat than non-metals.

14. (B)
Wood is a bad conductor of heat.

16. (D)
The molecules of liquids and gases are not rigidly bound to each other and can move freely. This makes transfer of heat by convection possible.

26. (D)	27. (B)	28. (C)	29. (B)	30. (D)	31 (D)	32. (A)	33. (D)	34. (A)	35. (B)

28. (C)

The upper fixed point in the Celsius scale is 100°C, which is the boiling point of water.

29. (B)

Gases expand the most upon heating because of the large intermolecular distances and less intermolecular force. Carbon dioxide being a gas will expand the most.

30. (D)

A medium (solid) is required for conduction to take place.

31. (D)

Though substances contract on cooling. water expand when cooled beyond 4°C. This is known as anomalous behaviour of water.

32. (A)

Human beings are warm blooded, which means that their body temperature has to be maintained around a particular temperature which is 37°C or 98° F. Water plays an important role in this.

4. ACIDS, BASES AND SALTS

Answer Key

1. (C)	2. (A)	3. (B)	4. (B)	5. (C)	6. (C)	7. (A)	8. (B)	9. (C)	10. (D)
11. (C)	12. (B)	13. (D)	14. (A)	15. (C)	16. (B)	17. (A)	18. (D)	19. (D)	20. (D)
21. (B)	22. (C)	23. (B)	24. (B)	25. (C)					

14. (A)

Because of the tremendous heat liberated always acids are added to water and not vice versa.

17. (A)

KOH (Potassium hydroxide) is the common name of caustic potash.

19. (D)

When acid reacts with metal it forms salt + H_2

22. (C)

In acidic medium methyl orange turns red in colour.

23. (B)

In basic medium methyl orange turns yellow in colour.

24. (D)

Acids are sour and corrosive and turns blue litmus red. When the oxides of non-metals dissolve in water they form acids. Oxides of non-metals are acidic in nature.

HOTS (ACHIEVERS SECTION)

26. (A)	27. (B)	28. (A)	29. (D)	30. (B)

26. (B)

Calcium is more reactive than hydrogen.

29. (D)

Magnesium is more reactive than zinc.

5. PHYSICAL AND CHEMICAL CHANGES

Answer Key

1. (B)	2. (A)	3. (C)	4. (D)	5. (A)	6. (B)	7. (D)	8. (B)	9. (A)	10. (D)
11. (D)	12. (C)	13. (A)	14. (B)	15. (A)	16. (C)	17. (B)	18. (A)	19. (C)	20. (A)
21. (C)	22. (C)	23. (A)	24. (C)	25. (B)	26. (A)	27. (C)	28. (B)	29. (B)	30. (D)

3. (C)
Acid rain occurs mainly because of carbon dioxide, sulphur dioxide and nitrogen dioxide which are all pollutants.

4. (D)
This is a physical change even though the characteristics of this mixture is different from the original substances can retain their properties and can be got back easily.

7. (D)
All chemical changes are irreversible and the original substances can not be obtained.

11. (D)
No new substances are formed in all these changes.

12. (C)
The soil is acidic and should be neutralized by adding slaked lime (calcium hydroxide) which is a base.

14. (B)
The candle started melting, but since no new substance was formed it is a physical change.

17. (B)
Magnesium hydroxide or $Mg(OH)_2$ is an antacid. It is also known as milk of magnesia. It neutralizes excess HCl (acid) present in stomach

21. (C)
Both salt and water are neutral towards litmus.

22. (C)
Z is either water or salt, both of which can be obtained from the reaction between acid and a salt. Since X is a base and Y is an acid, Z can be obtained from the reaction between X and Y.

25. (B)
The chemical name of slaked lime is calcium hydroxide and calcium oxide is the chemical name of quick lime.

26. (A)
Since, no new substances are formed in this change, it is a physical change.

HOTS (ACHIEVERS SECTION)

31. (D)	32. (A)	33. (C)	34. (D)	35. (D)

31. (D)
Here, only a change of state from liquid and solid to gas is seen, and no new substances are formed

32. (A)
The candle started melting, but since no new substance was formed, it is a physical change.

Answer Key

1. (D)	2. (B)	3. (C)	4. (B)	5. (C)	6. (B)	7. (A)	8. (D)	9. (D)	10. (C)
11. (C)	12. (C)	13. (B)	14. (C)	15. (B)	16. (D)	17. (D)	18. (B)	19. (A)	20. (D)
21. (B)	22. (C)	23. (D)	24. (B)	25. (A)					

4. (B)
Arboreal animals or animals living on trees have strong claws and broad hip girdles and spines to prevent them from slipping and have ability to climb up the trees.

9. (D)
White colour, thick skin and lots of fat are features of adaptation in penguins in cold climate.

12. (C)
Red eyed frog has sticky pads on its feet to climb the trees.

15. (B)
Opposable thumb helps in holding the branch. It is an adaptation to arboreal life or tree dwelling animals.

HOTS (ACHIEVERS SECTION)

26. (C)	27. (A)	28. (B)	29. (C)	30. (B)

26. (C)
The streamlined body of fish helps it to swim, gills to breath underwater and scales to reduce water resistence while swimming.

7. WINDS, STORMS AND CYCLONES

Answer Key

1. (C)	2. (D)	3. (A)	4. (C)	5. (B)	6. (D)	7. (D)	8. (A)	9. (D)	10. (A)
11. (A)	12. (B)	13. (C)	14. (C)	15. (B)	16. (D)	17. (B)	18. (B)	19. (B)	20. (A)
21. (B)	22. (D)	23. (B)	24. (B)	25. (A)					

1. (C)
Warmer air rises higher. This is because gases expand when they are heated.

4. (C)
When a wind flows very fast, a low pressure is produced temporarily which is filled by the rushing wind nearby.

6. (D)
Upon heating, the molecules in the gases go further away from each other and thus become lighter.

7. (D)
The winds coming from the southwest blow over the Indian ocean and bring lots of rains.

8. (A)
The energy contained in the gaseous form (vapour) is more than the energy contained in the liquid form (water), therefore when vapour changes to water it loses some heat.

10. (A)

Salinity is harmful to the plants. During cyclones, the sea waves rise high and flood the land making the soil saline (infertile).

11. (A)

Even when the cyclone is very far, strong winds push water towards the shore causing huge water waves.

13. (C)

Sea and land breezes are caused because of an uneven heating of the earth and through convection currents.

14. (C)

A ball falls down to the ground because of gravity.

15. (B)

Because of the curved upper surface of the aeroplane more air flows in the same time as compared to the lower surface. Therefore, the pressure over the aeroplane is less when compared to the lower surface.

18. (B)

When we suck into the straw, a low pressure is created in it, which makes the higher pressure in the bottle to push the drink into the straw.

20. (A)

When winds blow over a weak roof, it creates a low pressure over it and a high pressure inside causing the roof to be blown off. Opening the doors and windows reduces this pressure difference and avoids the roof from being blown off.

21. (B)

Wind that are cold usually show lateral (sideways) movement while the one that are warm show vertical movement. Since the winds blow from the north and the south towards the equator it must be hotter than the other places.

HOTS (ACHIEVERS SECTION)

26. (B)	27. (C)	28. (C)	29. (D)	30. (B)

27. (C)

Cyclone are called as Willy-Willy in Australia, Huricane in South China sea and Tornado in U.S.A. Temperate cyclone is caused in higher latitudes due to frontal system of air masses and is different from tropical cyclones.

28. (C)

Sea and land breezes are caused because of an uneven heating of the earth and through convection currents.

8. NATURAL RESOURCES AND THEIR CONSERVATION

Answer Key

1. (B)	2. (B)	3. (D)	4. (C)	5. (B)	6. (A)	7. (C)	8. (A)	9. (C)	10. (B)
11. (A)	12. (D)	13. (D)	14. (B)	15. (A)	16. (C)	17. (C)	18. (B)	19. (B)	20. (C)
21. (B)	22. (C)	23. (D)	24. (B)	25. (D)					

3. (D)

The water table of a place depends on the rainfall and water seepage.

8. (A)

The microorganisms which convert the dead plants and animals to humus are known as decomposers.

17. (C)

Green plants trap solar energy and synthesize their food, all animals directly or indirectly depends upon plants hence a food chain will not begin in the absence of green plants.

18. (B)

Roots of trees normally bind the soil together

HOTS (ACHIEVERS SECTION)

26. (C)	27. (A)	28. (B)	29. (D)	30. (C)

9. RESPIRATION IN ORGANISMS

Answer Key

1. (A)	2. (B)	3. (C)	4. (B)	5. (A)	6. (C)	7. (A)	8. (B)	9. (C)	10. (C)
11. (D)	12. (A)	13. (B)	14. (D)	15. (C)	16. (C)	17. (B)	18. (D)	19. (A)	20. (B)
21. (C)	22. (C)	23. (C)	24. (D)	25. (B)	26. (C)	27. (A)	28. (B)	29. (C)	30. (A)

7. (A)

In man nostrils are analogus to spiracles, through nostrils air enters into nasal cavity. Nostrils consists of fine air and lined with mucus. Hair filters the air from dust particles.

9. (C)

Respiratory membrane should be semipermeable to allow exchange of gases.

13. (B)

The actual site of gaseous exchange in respiratory system is alveoli. Alveolus are richly supplied with blood capillaries permeable membrane which allows exchange of gases through it.

17. (B)

Gills are the respiratory organs in aquatic animals. Gills are richly supplied with blood vessels when water enters into the bronchial chamber dissolved oxygen from the water is absorbed.

20. (B)

Lactic acid accumulation leads to muscle fatigue. It is also called as muscle cramp, due to the insufficient supply of oxygen.

HOTS (ACHIEVERS SECTION)

31. (B)	32. (C)	33. (D)	34. (D)	35. (C)

33. (D)

The actual site of gaseous exchange in respiratory system is Alveoli. Alveolus are richly supplied with blood capillaries permeable membrane which allows exchange of gases through it.

OLYMPIAD WORKBOOK (NSO) CLASS– 7

10. TRANSPORTATION AND EXCRETION

Answer Key

1. (B)	2. (B)	3. (A)	4. (A)	5. (B)	6. (C)	7. (A)	8. (D)	9. (B)	10. (A)
11. (B)	12. (C)	13. (A)	14. (B)	15. (D)	16. (A)	17. (B)	18. (C)	19. (C)	20. (C)
21. (D)	22. (B)	23. (C)	24. (D)	25. (A)					

7. (A)
Capillaries have no muscular wall. They have thin walls hence diffusion or exchange of gases takes place in capillaries easily.

8. (D)
Transpiration means the loss of water and waste materials through stomata and lenticels.

16. (A)
The droplets of water arranged at the edges of leaves or flower in the morning is due to water transpired from stomata and lenticels.

17. (B)
Plant cells store waste materials in their vacuoles. However, plants also store waste materials. But in the bark. It comes out as gum, or resin. Some leaves store waste in the form of latex.

23. (C)
Osmosis is the flow of water molecules from the region of higher water pressure to lower water pressure through a semipermeable membrane is called osmosis.

HOTS (ACHIEVERS SECTION)

26. (A)	27. (D)	28. (D)	29. (C)	30. (C)

11. REPRODUCTION IN PLANTS

Answer Key

1. (A)	2. (B)	3. (C)	4. (C)	5. (A)	6. (D)	7. (A)	8. (C)	9. (B)	10. (C)
11. (C)	12. (D)	13. (C)	14. (B)	15. (A)	16. (D)	17. (B)	18. (A)	19. (B)	20. (C)
21. (A)	22. (B)	23. (C)	24. (B)	25. (C)	26. (B)	27. (D)	28. (A)	29. (B)	30. (D)

3. (C)
Spores are the reproductive structures in some fungi and plants. These are tiny structures protected by thick walls to survive unfavorable conditions.

9. (B)
Mushrooms reproduce by asexual reproduction through spores. It is the most common method of reproduction is Mushrooms.

10. (C)
Bryophyllum develops from buds on the modified leaves. Buds are developed on the leaf margin at notches. These when seperated grow into a new plant.

16. (D)

The rapidly reproducing yeast cells by budding release carbon dioxide due to anaerobic respiration in the dough. Hence, the dough rises.

17. (B)

Stigma, style and ovary constitute the female part of flower.

18. (A)

Flowers with stamens or roecium and pistils or gynoecium or male and female reproductive organs are called as complete flowers.

23. (C)

The seeds of balsam fruit are dry and dispersed by explosion due to the touch of our hands. The walls of the fruit coil inwards, creating forces that throws the seeds to a distance.

HOTS (ACHIEVERS SECTION)

| 31. (A) | 32. (D) | 33. (D) | 34. (C) | 35. (C) |

12. MOTION AND TIME

Answer Key

1. (C)	2. (B)	3. (C)	4. (D)	5. (D)	6. (B)	7. (A)	8. (B)	9. (C)	10. (A)
11. (A)	12. (A)	13. (D)	14. (B)	15. (C)	16. (A)	17. (C)	18. (D)	19. (C)	20. (D)

3. (C)

Mean solar day $= 24$ h $= 24 \times 60 \times 60$
$$= 86400 \text{ seconds}$$

4. (D)

In a constant speed the change in position of the body remains the same for a particular interval of time. Divide time axis into small parts and see the distance travelled in each of these parts is the same in choices A, B and C (zero in 'C'). But the distance changes in 'D'.

7. (A)

$$1 \text{ km/h} = \frac{5}{18} \text{ m/s}$$

$$\therefore \quad 180 \text{ km/h} = 180 \times \frac{5}{18} = 50 \text{ m/s}$$

8. (B)

A fan shows circular motion.

9. (C)

An odometer measures distances.

12. (A)

The time taken by P is the lowest among the four, because more is the area under the wine, greater is the speed. Hence, P is the fastest.

13. (D)

60 min $= 1$ hour

$$5 \text{ min} = \frac{1}{60} \times 5 = \frac{1}{12} \text{ hour}$$

$$\text{Speed} = \frac{\text{distance}}{\text{time}} = \frac{5}{1/12} = 5 \times 12 = 60 \text{ km/hr}$$

14. (B)

A light year is the distance covered by light in one year, so it is the unit of distance and not of time.

15. (C)

Speed is the change of position of the body with respect to time. From the graph it can be seen that the change becomes less with time till there is no change at all i.e. till the speed becomes zero.

17. (C)

$$20 \text{ min} = 20 \times 60 \text{ seconds}$$
$$= 1200 \text{ seconds}$$
$$\text{Distance} = \text{speed} \times \text{time}$$
$$= 3 \times 1200$$
$$= 3.6 \text{ km} \ (1000 \text{ m} = 1 \text{ km})$$

19. (C)

$$1000 \text{ m} = 1 \text{ km}$$

$$1 \text{ m} = \frac{1}{1000} \text{ km}$$
$$3600 \text{ s} = 1 \text{ hr or } 1 \text{ s} = \frac{1}{3600} \text{ hr}$$
$$20 \text{ m/s} = 20 \times \frac{1}{1000} \text{ km} \times \frac{3600}{1} \text{ hr}$$
$$= 72 \text{ km/hr}$$

HOTS (ACHIEVERS SECTION)

21. (D)	22. (B)	23. (A)	24. (C)	25. (B)

22. (B)

In a uniform speed, the change in position of the body remains the same for a particular interval of time. The distance travelled in option (A), (C) and (D) is the same, in (C) it is zero. But the distance changes in option (B). Hence, the answer is (B).

23. (A)

$$\text{Time} = 15 \text{ minutes} = \frac{15}{60} \text{ hour} = \frac{1}{4} \text{ hour}$$
$$\text{distance} = 8 \text{ km}$$
$$\text{Speed} = \frac{\text{distance}}{\text{time}} = \frac{8 \text{ km}}{1/4 \text{ hour}}$$
$$= 8 \times 4 \text{ km/hour} = 32 \text{ km/h}$$

13. ELECTRIC CURRENT AND ITS EFFECTS

Answer Key

1. (B)	2. (A)	3. (D)	4. (B)	5. (B)	6. (C)	7. (A)	8. (C)	9. (A)	10. (A)
11. (C)	12. (B)	13. (C)	14. (D)	15. (C)	16. (C)	17. (C)	18. (C)	19. (A)	20. (D)
21. (A)	22. (D)	23. (B)	24. (B)	25. (C)					

4. (B)

Silver is a metal and a good conductor of electricity.

5. (B)

The chemical energy stored in two cells is more than one. The electrical energy used by one bulb is less than the energy used by two bulbs. So the bulb in the circuit that has one bulb and two cells will glow the brightest.

7. (A)

Plastic is good insulator of electricity and makes it possible to work with wires without any harm/injury.

9. (A)

An open key does not allow current to flow in the circuit.

13. (C)

It is a temporary magnet which works only in the presence of electricity.

17. (C)

Using a cork in the circuit will break it, since it is an insulator. Removing one of the cells will reduce the flow of electricity and make the bulbs dimmer.

18. (C)

Silver is also better conductor, nonmagnetic but expensive material.

23. (B)

Because of too many cells, the electricity that was flowing through the filament of the bulb was more, causing it to melt and break

HOTS (ACHIEVERS SECTION)

26. (C)	27. (A)	28. (D)	29. (B)	30. (A)

27. (A)

A heater is used to obtain heat energy. For light energy, a bulb or other sources are used.

14. LIGHT

Answer Key

1. (A)	2. (C)	3. (D)	4. (D)	5. (B)	6. (B)	7. (B)	8. (D)	9. (A)	10. (C)
11. (D)	12. (B)	13. (C)	14. (C)	15. (C)	16. (C)	17. (D)	18. (B)	19. (B)	20. (D)
21. (A)	22. (B)	23. (C)	24. (A)	25. (B)	26. (B)	27. (C)	28. (D)	29. (D)	30. (A)

5. (B)

Earth is a non-luminous body and does not emit any light.

7. (B)

The speed of light decreases with an increase in the density of the medium.

10. (C)

T is a laterally symmetrical object and hence its image in a plane mirror would be the same as itself.

12. (B)

The energy of the light keeps on getting absorbed and transformed as it moves through a medium. Therefore, its intensity decreases.

26. (B)

During the same time the ratio of the height and length of any object will be equal to that of any other including 'x'.

Step 1 - Let the height of the tree be 'h'. The length of the tree is given as 'L'

∴ the ratio of its height and length would be $\dfrac{h}{L}$

Step 2 - This ratio will be the same as 'x'

∴ $\dfrac{h}{L} = x$ or $h = x \times L$

28. (D)

This happens due to a phenomenon called persistence of vision.

HOTS (ACHIEVERS SECTION)

31. (A)	32. (B)	33. (B)	34. (C)	35. (D)	36. (A)	37. (A)	38. (D)	39. (C)	40. (B)

36. (A)

Let the height of the flag pole be 'h'

The length of the light pole = 25 m

The constant ratio of length of object to its shadow = 2.5 (given)

$$\therefore \quad \frac{h}{25} = 2.5 \Rightarrow h = 2.5 \times 25 = 62.5 \text{ m}$$

37. (A)

Concave mirrors, plane mirrors always form images of same size as that of the object.

38. (D)

The chemical energy stored in two cells is more than in one cell. The electrical energy used by one bulb is less than the energy used by two bulbs. So, the bulb in the circuit that has one bulb and two cells will glow the brightest.

15. LOGICAL REASONING

Answer Key

1. (C)	2. (A)	3. (B)	4. (A)	5. (D)	6. (C)	7. (A)	8. (C)	9. (C)	10. (D)
11. (D)	12. (A)	13. (A)	14. (A)	15. (C)	16. (C)	17. (A)	18. (D)	19. (D)	20. (A)
21. (C)	22. (C)	23. (A)	24. (C)	25. (C)	26. (A)	27. (C)	28. (A)	29. (B)	30. (A)
31. (A)	32. (C)	33. (A)	34. (D)	35. (B)	36. (A)	37. (C)	38. (A)	39. (B)	40. (C)
41. (C)	42. (A)	43. (B)	44. (D)	45. (A)					

1. (C)

$7 \times 5 + 6 = 41$

$8 \times 7 + 5 = 61$

$6 \times 7 + 9 = 51$

2. (A)

$7 \times 4 + 3 \times 5 = 28 + 15 = 43$

$6 \times 2 + 6 \times 4 = 12 + 24 = 36$

$9 \times 3 + 5 \times 7 = 27 + 35 = 62$

3. (B)

$84 \div 7 + 42 \div 2 = 12 + 21 = 33$

$117 \div 13 + 96 \div 16 = 9 + 6 = 15$

$153 \div 17 + 63 \div 3 = 9 + 21 = 30$

4. (A)

This is a simple division series. Each number is divided by 5.

5. (D)

In this simple subtraction series, each number decreases by 0.4.

6. (C)

This is a simple multiplication series. Each number is 3 times more than the previous number.

7. (A)

The series is mopn/mopn/mopn/mopn. Thus, the pattern 'mopn' is repeated.

8. (C)

The series is bbccaa/ccaabb/aabbcc. Thus, the letter pairs move in a cyclic order.

9. (C)

The series is man/man/man/man/man. Thus, the pattern 'man' is repeated.

10. (D)

Each of the numbers is a prime number except 12.

11. (D)

Each of the numbers except 81 is a prime number.

12. (A)

In each number except 751, the difference of third and first digit is the middle one.

13. (A)

Each letter in the word is moved thirteen steps forward to obtain the corresponding letter of the code.

14. (A)

Each letter in the word is moved one step forward to obtain the corresponding letter of the code.

15. (C)

Each letter in the word is moved three steps forward to obtain the corresponding letter of the code.

16. (C)

waiting, wanting, watching, waving.

17. (A)

Lapse, Laurel, Leave, Leisure.

18. (D)

Project, Property, Protein, Proverb.

19. (D)

Because, wife of husband - herself; Brother of daughter - son. So, the man is Ritu's son.

20. (A)

Grandmother is one female, mother is another, wives of four sons are the four females and two daughters of all four sons are eight females. So, in all there are $1 + 1 + 4 + 8 = 14$ females.

21. (C)

Shalu is Mona's step-daughter, which means Shalu is the daughter of the other wife of Ravi. So, Shalu is the daughter of Leena or Leena is the mother of Shalu.

22. (C)

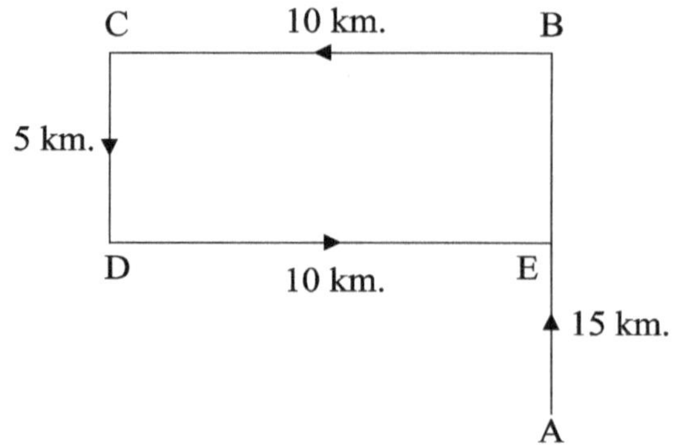

Therefore, it is clear that Lokesh is in the North from his house.

23. (A)

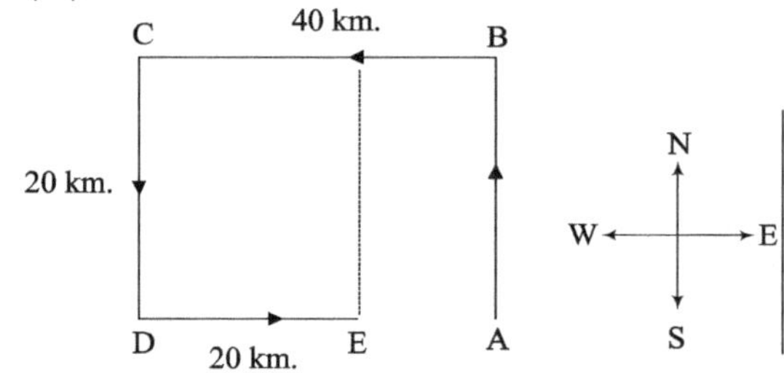

Required distance $= BC - DE = 40 - 20$
$$= 20 \text{ km}$$

24. (C)

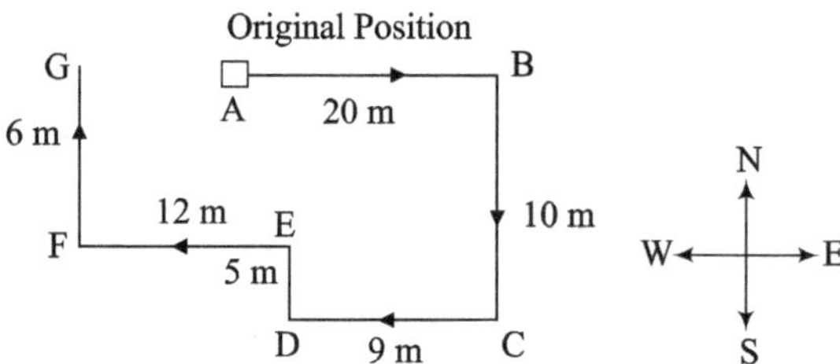

Therefore, it is clear that Sundar will face towards North.

25. (C)

5 7 8 9 7 6 5 3 4 2 6 8 9 7 5 2 4 6 2 9 7 6 4 7

8 9 7 6

26. (A)

2, 5, 8 all have frequency 3.

27. (C)

7 has highest frequency.

28. (A)

All other figures can be rotated into each other.

29. (B)

In each one of the figures except figure (2), three cups open towards the pentagon and two cups open outwards.

30. (A)

All other figures can be rotated into each other.

31. (A)

The letters of the adjacent faces to the face with letter A are B, F, C and E. Hence D is the letter of the face opposite to the face with letter (A).

32. (C)

According to the rule (2), when 3 points are at the bottom then 4 points will be at the top.

33. (A)

Here one of the two common faces (5) is in the same position, then according to the rule (2), the remaining face with the 4 dots will be opposite to face with dots 2.

43. (B)

All the three are different professions.

44. (D)

Product and Machinery are different from each other but both are found in Factory.

45. (A)

All mothers are women and some mothers and some women may be engineers.

MODEL TEST PAPER

Answer Key

1. (B)	2. (C)	3. (B)	4. (C)	5. (C)	6. (C)	7. (D)	8. (B)	9. (C)	10. (A)
11. (A)	12. (B)	13. (C)	14. (C)	15. (C)	16. (B)	17. (B)	18. (B)	19. (C)	20. (D)
21. (B)	22. (D)	23. (B)	24. (C)	25. (D)	26. (A)	27. (A)	28. (D)	29. (B)	30. (D)
31. (C)	32. (B)	33. (C)	34. (C)	35. (B)	36. (A)	37. (D)	38. (C)	39. (C)	40. (A)
41. (D)	42. (B)	43. (D)	44. (C)	45. (B)	46. (A)	47. (B)	48. (C)	49. (C)	50. (C)

SAMPLE OMR ANSWER SHEET

1. STUDENT NAME (IN ENGLISH CAPITAL LETTERS ONLY)

Students must write and darken the respective circles completely using HB Pencil only. Othewise their Answer Sheets will not be evaluated.

PERSONAL DETAILS

2. SCHOOL CODE

3. CLASS

4. SECTION

5. ROLL NO.

6. QUESTION PAPER SET

A ○
B ○
C ○
D ○

7. MOBILE NUMBER

8. GENDER

MALE ○
FEMALE ○

9. STREAM
(Only for Class XI and XII Students)

MATHEMATICS ○
BIOLOGY ○
OTHERS ○

MARK YOUR ANSWERS

No.	A	B	C	D	No.	A	B	C	D
1.	A	B	C	D	26.	A	B	C	D
2.	A	B	C	D	27.	A	B	C	D
3.	A	B	C	D	28.	A	B	C	D
4.	A	B	C	D	29.	A	B	C	D
5.	A	B	C	D	30.	A	B	C	D
6.	A	B	C	D	31.	A	B	C	D
7.	A	B	C	D	32.	A	B	C	D
8.	A	B	C	D	33.	A	B	C	D
9.	A	B	C	D	34.	A	B	C	D
10.	A	B	C	D	35.	A	B	C	D
11.	A	B	C	D	36.	A	B	C	D
12.	A	B	C	D	37.	A	B	C	D
13.	A	B	C	D	38.	A	B	C	D
14.	A	B	C	D	39.	A	B	C	D
15.	A	B	C	D	40.	A	B	C	D
16.	A	B	C	D	41.	A	B	C	D
17.	A	B	C	D	42.	A	B	C	D
18.	A	B	C	D	43.	A	B	C	D
19.	A	B	C	D	44.	A	B	C	D
20.	A	B	C	D	45.	A	B	C	D
21.	A	B	C	D	46.	A	B	C	D
22.	A	B	C	D	47.	A	B	C	D
23.	A	B	C	D	48.	A	B	C	D
24.	A	B	C	D	49.	A	B	C	D
25.	A	B	C	D	50.	A	B	C	D

Signature of the Student & Date of Examination

Signature of the Invigilator & Date of Examination

V&S Publishers, F-2/16 Ansari Road, Daryaganj, New Delhi-110002, ☎ 011-23240026-27
✉ info@vspublishers.com, 🌐 www.vspublishers.com

www.ingramcontent.com/pod-product-compliance
Lightning Source LLC
LaVergne TN
LVHW080600200726

843510LV00004B/970